Your Towns and Cities in the

❖

Isle of Man
in the Great War

Caroline Smith was born and educated in Wakefield, West Yorkshire, and has a degree in history from Lancaster University. After taking an accountancy qualification and working mainly in manufacturing, Caroline and her husband relocated to the Isle of Man.

Caroline is the author of several articles about the island. She is also involved with the local History in Action group, who aim to tell the stories of the island, including those of the Great War, through drama.

Your Towns and Cities in the Great War

Isle of Man
in the Great War

Caroline Smith

Pen & Sword
MILITARY

First published in Great Britain in 2014 by
PEN & SWORD MILITARY
an imprint of
Pen and Sword Books Ltd
47 Church Street
Barnsley
South Yorkshire S70 2AS

Copyright © Caroline Smith, 2014

ISBN 978 1 78383 122 7

Printed and bound in England
by Page Bros, Norwich

Typeset in Times New Roman by Chic Graphics

Pen & Sword Books Ltd incorporates the imprints of
Pen & Sword Archaeology, Atlas, Aviation, Battleground, Discovery,
Family History, History, Maritime, Military, Naval, Politics, Railways,
Select, Social History, Transport, True Crime, Claymore Press,
Frontline Books, Leo Cooper, Praetorian Press, Remember When,
Seaforth Publishing and Wharncliffe.

For a complete list of Pen and Sword titles please contact
Pen and Sword Books Limited
47 Church Street, Barnsley, South Yorkshire, S70 2AS, England
E-mail: enquiries@pen-and-sword.co.uk
Website: www.pen-and-sword.co.uk

Contents

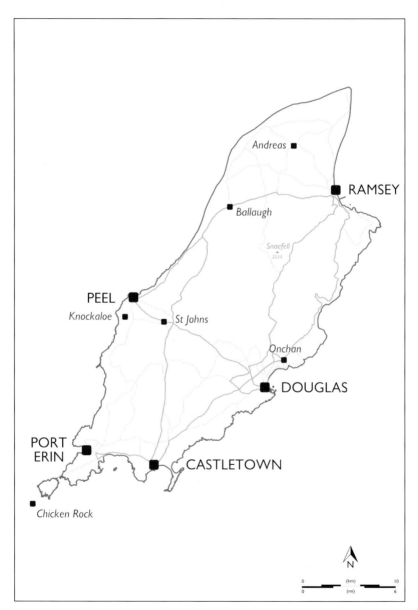

Map of Isle of Man. Courtesy of Dan Karran.

Introduction

Nestled off the coasts of Scotland and Cumbria, in the northern Irish Sea, lies the Isle of Man. This small island, only 221 square miles, is known today for the TT Races and for being a financial centre.

In 1914 the population of the island was about 50,000 and the main industry was tourism. Between Whit week and the end of September hundreds of thousands of tourists, many from Lancashire, flocked to the island for a holiday.

The season of 1914 looked as if it would be the best ever and it was in full swing when war brought that to an abrupt halt. While those dependent on the season faced an uncertain financial future, others, notably farmers, would become wealthy. This growing financial division would play its part in the increasing social tensions of war time.

Politically, the island did not have the independence that it does today. Legislation in the latter half of the nineteenth century had given the island more freedom to manage its own affairs, but the British Government and Crown appointed Governor still had much influence.

Just as in the Houses of Parliament in London, the Manx parliament has an upper and lower house. The lower house, or House of Keys, has twenty-four elected members or MHKs. The upper house, or Legislative Council, has ten members. At the time of the First World War these were appointed and the Lieutenant Governor presided over them. To pass legislation the two houses meet in a full parliament called Tynwald.

Every year on 5 July, there is an open-air ceremony at St John's where all the Acts passed by Tynwald during the preceding year are proclaimed to the assembled crowd in both Manx Gaelic and English. The Tynwald Day ceremony, which has taken place for over a thousand

Douglas War Memorial.

years, is not only a national holiday but also the chance for the islanders to present grievances for the attention of the government.

In the early years of the twentieth century there were many on the island who hoped to see British influence recede and the power of the Governor reduced. There were also calls for reform, particularly of the unaccountable Legislative Council. The British Government had already reported on reform for the island and they were receptive to the principles, however the Manx Government, under the leadership of the Governor, had been very slow to put any changes in place.

In 1902, Lord Raglan, a distinguished military man, became Governor. Unfortunately, he displayed hostility towards the Keys and, as an ultra conservative, he was often at odds with the Liberal Government in England. This recipe for conflict came to a head during the war. The failure to implement social policy in line with England and an unreformed Legislative Council where self interest ruled, were among the many grievances held against him.

When war came to the island, it gave the impetus to those who were most affected by it to demand reform, both socially and politically. By the time peace was declared the pro-reformists were seeing positive steps being taken towards their aims. The battle had been bitter and brought many divisions to the island.

Of the 50,000 population, over 8000 Manxmen served their country. This represented eighty-two per cent of the island's males of military age. Few places gave so high a percentage of their men and over a thousand of these would never return. This is the story of the people they left behind.

Note to reader – all government accounts figures are in accordance with Samuel Norris.

Acknowledgements
I would like to extend my many thanks to the staff at the Manx Museum and *i*Museum, who have been most helpful, and also to cartographer Dan Karran www.dankarran.com.

CHAPTER 1

1914
Eager for a Fight

Officially war was declared on Tuesday, 4 August 1914. However, two days before, the towns of the Isle of Man witnessed what the *Peel City Guardian*, a local paper, called 'the first omen of trouble'. In full view of the patriotic crowds that had gathered, the island's Royal Naval Reservists were called up.

When the west coast city of Peel had been in its prime, this would have been a disaster. Fishing had been the main industry and, as a majority of fishermen were reservists, it would have meant its virtual paralysis. Fishing, though, had been in decline since the 1890s. With fewer men turning to it, it did not suffer as badly in 1914 as it might have done. Even so, the town still lost a large number of men who were hurried out to join various posts of duty.

Despite the impending loss of many of Peel's men, the city was in a state of excitement, with just about every resident taking to the station or the quayside to give the local reservists a hearty send-off. Such was the fever that church was almost forgotten as so many wanted to shake the hands of the men departing, sing patriotic songs and cheer them on their way.

Similarly, in the north of the island, the town of Ramsey also witnessed a large call up. The Reverend M.W. Harrison remarked in his sermon that the scene in the market place, only a few minutes previously, was 'an unparalleled event' in the town's history.

In Douglas, the Bishop of Sodor and Man preached an open-air sermon to a congregation of holiday makers, estimated by local papers to number 10,000. He warned that England would almost certainly be drawn into war because of obligations to her allies. His rousing words claimed that any man not willing to 'shoulder a musket' for King and country was not worthy of the name. He invited his congregation to show their patriotism and sing the national anthem, which they did, willingly.

Not everyone, though, was so enthusiastic. Back in Peel, the Reverend F.E. Watson was busy preaching his condemnation of modern society as 'unchristian'. He claimed the evidence was there in the European crisis that the church had not prevented. Such pacifism, though, would be a small voice drowned out by the general war cry. After all, if war did come, it would all be over in a few weeks, having been a great adventure.

Few would have predicted the course that history was to take.

Two days later, when war was officially declared, the Isle of Man was in the midst of a very successful summer season. Since the 1830s the island had attracted tourists, and by the 1860s this had become very lucrative.

The 1913 season had been of particular note. The number of tourists, 635,000 of them, had surpassed all previous records. As the island's population at the time was only about 50,000, such a large number of visitors was very important to the island's economy, as they all had to be fed, housed and entertained for the duration of their stay.

The season of 1914 held all the promise of surpassing the previous year. There were around 2000 boarding houses in Douglas alone, and they were full. The dance halls were packed and the music-hall stars of the era were booked to perform. Among them was Florrie Forde. Famous for her voice, which could fill any theatre without amplification and her rapid costume changes, she had become the 'darling of Douglas'. She had performed for a number of years, and it is said that she sang 'Tipperary' at the Derby Castle Theatre. After this, so the story goes, a group of soldiers sang it as they left the island and it soon became one of the most famous marching songs of the era.

The island had been buzzing with the holiday spirit, but war brought that abruptly to an end. There was a general mass exodus as people were in a hurry to return home and, where possible, join up. It was not just tourists leaving either. Their entertainers, too, some of whom were of German descent, and possibly unsure of their position, were anxious to quit the island.

Of the entertainment that remained, the orchestra playing at the Villa Marina was obliged to change its name. The 'Imperial Vienna Orchestra' just did not sound patriotic. Similarly, it was only thought correct to remove the German-sounding word 'Kursaal' from the Villa's entertainment complex.

The popular Mr New's Band, a group of Bavarian musicians, were among the entertainers who left. They had had a long standing arrangement to be paid £10 for the season but, with the outbreak of hostilities, they had quickly removed from the island. Being unable to communicate with friends in Germany, they found themselves stranded in London and in financial difficulties. They appealed for their pay and it was agreed, as long as the Governor approved, that as they had worked for half the season they could be paid £5.

Up to the outbreak of war, Mr New's Band had been well advertised and praised. The newspapers commented on how everyone was looking forward to hearing them play. Such was their appeal that there had been a new bandstand built for them. Their swift departure left a hole in the entertainment programme that was filled by a local Ramsey band. The band from Ramsey was thanked for its efforts and the expressions of praise, made only a few days earlier, for various foreign entertainment groups turned to scathing comments of how the island had been saved the 'pain' of listening to enemy musicians.

The island was still a hive of activity but the focus had changed. Instead of tourists seeking entertainment, it was local men who were responding to recruitment drives. They queued each day at the recruiting office which, under the charge of Major Hamilton, had opened above Parr's Bank on Prospect Hill, Douglas.

There was no military presence on the island in 1914 except for the Isle of Man Volunteers and the Officers' Training Corps at King William College. The Volunteers were called up as part of the mobilization of the Territorial Forces on 5 August. They were put to work guarding the sub-marine telegraph cable and war signal stations; and later would guard the camps, government offices, the Post Office and, at times, the harbours. To some this would no doubt be a great disappointment as they were hoping to be sent overseas to join the 'real war'.

King William College and War Memorial, home to the Officers' Training Corps.

The Governor also authorized the formation of a national reserve called The Loyal Manx Association, which was made up of able-bodied men who for various reasons were not able to join the active forces. They were expected to learn to drill and shoot, be ready to relieve other men for active service and, if necessary, defend the island. In many ways they were an early form of the Home Guard.

For the islanders, the war, from the outset, was highly visible and they had an insatiable desire to know the latest news. The *Peel City Guardian* found its offices swamped daily and reported that 'before the papers were unpacked there was a wild raid on our premises, people fairly scrambling over each others' heads to obtain a paper, and our supplies have vanished altogether in the space of a few minutes.'

Amid the excitement, the panic and the flurry of activity as people left the island and men were recruited and trained, it is unlikely that many people were thinking far into the future. However, advice was being given and, among it, it was suggested that people should 'secure their stock of herrings' as the war was likely to increase food prices. The traditional curing of herring to make the local kippers was an industry now in danger of collapse. After the call up of the naval reserve the crews supplying the curing businesses in Port St Mary had been reduced from twenty-four to just ten. What the advisors probably did not realise was just how far food prices would rise over the next four years, how many foodstuffs would be affected and the consequences of this for the island.

While most people were trying to leave the island, there were several Manx ladies who, having found themselves caught in the wrong place at the wrong time, were anxious to return. For example, Miss Catherine Duke was in Belgium visiting a friend during the summer of 1914. When it became obvious that she had to return she found the trains already crowded with troops despite war not actually having been declared. When she reached the Channel all the boats to England had ceased to run. Luckily, the British Government had chartered the Canadian steamer *Montrose* to bring refugees back and Catherine was able to secure her crossing to England on the vessel.

Writing in the *Isle of Man Examiner* a week later, Catherine recalled that cabins were scarce as there were so many people on board. Some had to sleep out on deck and she had made herself comfortable in the Marconi room. The journey to the Thames took fifty-six hours as they were sometimes held up and they were towing two other Canadian Pacific boats including the *Montreal.* Despite the difficulties of the journey and the sober circumstances, there was much dancing, a concert and everyone was in the best of spirits. Perhaps the highlight of her journey was seeing the cabin occupied by Crippen in his attempt to escape to America.

A Peel lady, Miss Finnegan, was staying at a school in Bonn with some other girls when they were informed that war had broken out between Germany and Serbia. She witnessed the German mobilization and recalled how local residents put pots of coffee and baskets of bread out on tables lining the streets for the soldiers to help themselves. She noted the enthusiasm of the German soldier and their confidence that France would easily fall and victory secured before Britian could join in.

As soon as Britain declared her intentions the locals were angry. British subjects were given a certain period of time to leave or they would face arrest. Not knowing how long they had or what arrangements could be made for their departure, they turned first to the local police and then to the Red Cross. They packed and left almost immediately, taking only what was necessary as they were forbidden from taking their trunks.

As they tried to negotiate their way through crowded railway stations they passed many bands of troops and were even 'entertained' by soldiers who showed them their guns and bayonets. There was no distinction between first, second and third class during their journey and at one point they even had to travel in a cattle car. They finally reached London with no money and having spent four days on a journey that would normally take sixteen hours.

Arguably the most worrying experience was that of Dorothy Davidson, daughter of Douglas man, Reverend J. Davidson. She had been in Germany at the time of the declaration of war and was interned on the island of Deanholm. It was a couple of weeks before a Herr Myhre of the Baltic Shipping Association was able to secure her liberty and have her escorted to neutral territory. *Mona's Herald* printed the story that she had telegraphed her father from Malmo saying she intended to sail for Liverpool from Copenhagen. *The Herald* wished her well for the journey and hoped that she would escape the danger of mines that the 'dastardly' Germans had laid in the North Sea.

While these ladies returned, the overwhelming direction of travel was away from Manx shores. As tourists, musicians and new recruits were swiftly departing, a gap was appearing and, unsuspected by many of the island's residents, that gap would not be relieved for several years. It would become little short of a catastrophe for some, and be the source of much political agitation.

The number of visitors arriving on the island fell drastically at the beginning of August 1914. In fact, by 10 August the directors of the Steam Packet Company had decided, at a specially called meeting, to lay up three vessels, *Ben-my-Chree*, *Viking* and *Empress Queen*, with immediate effect.

Within weeks the Admiralty had requisitioned several of the Steam Packet vessels and had asked for plans of several more. By the end of the year the pre-war fleet was reduced from fifteen steamers to just four. Even if visitors wanted to travel to the island, their means of doing so was severely restricted.

Samuel Norris, a leading political reformer on the island at the time, noted the significance of this in his memoirs. 'The transfer of the Steam Packet Company's fleet of steamers brought home, as nothing else could, the fact that the island was at war on a world-wide scale, and that, whether for short or long time, there could be no industry for thousands of its people, and no financial return on the millions of capital hitherto employed in providing comforts and pleasure for holiday-makers.'

These words were written over a decade later. It is unlikely that in 1914 Samuel Norris and his friends were as acutely aware of the problem they faced as his retrospective words suggest. Consequently, the mood of the island was still generally optimistic.

Tourists had left, but there were reports that some had returned to continue their holidays as they had found, once home, that there was not any real cause for alarm. Some of the various galas and events held around the island in the late summer season were still reasonably well patronised but others, such as the swimming gala, sports and visitors' concert in aid of the Peel Lifeboat were cancelled. The RNLI at Peel did ask instead for people to support the sale of 'Lifeboat buttonholes', which raised a satisfactory £17.

The *Ramsey Courier* even went as far as to say that there was reason to suppose that, as continental resorts were closed by the war, Ramsey and other parts of the island would benefit from a revival of the season in September. Clearly the paper was confident of a swift and positive outcome of the conflict as, on the same day, it published a report saying that the horoscope of the German Emperor had been cast three years before. Under the headline 'Germany Doomed', the paper said that the horoscope had foretold that Wilhelm II would be the last German Emperor, that the house of Hohenzollern would fall, and that if there was war between France and Germany, France would be victorious.

Although the horoscope would prove accurate, the optimism and frivolity of the paper in mid-August 1914 would be woefully misplaced. By the end of the season, officially 30 September, the number of visitors to the island had been just over 400,000. The dip in visitor numbers was unfortunate for those whose incomes relied on the industry of the season. It certainly made life hard for them but was probably sustainable for one year. The problem was that the war did not last for just one year. Instead it lasted long enough to bring financial ruin to one sizable, and important, sector of the island.

Another industry in steep decline at this time was mining. The Isle of Man has a number of mineral veins and, with advances in technology the mining of them was a profitable business in the eighteenth and nineteenth centuries. There had been several mines on the island but in 1914 only one remained: The Great Laxey Mine.

By the early twentieth century, after problems of mismanagement and strikes, the mine was also facing problems of a fluctuating metal market making the viability of mining unstable. Even selling the ore from the mines was becoming difficult. Many English smelting companies were stocking themselves with French, Italian and other foreign ores. The loss of most of the ability to ship the ores to England meant that much of it was simply stock piled. *Lady Isabella*, the massive water wheel that was used to pump water from the mine and

Lady Isabella, or the Laxey Wheel which still dominates the village and is a tourist attraction.

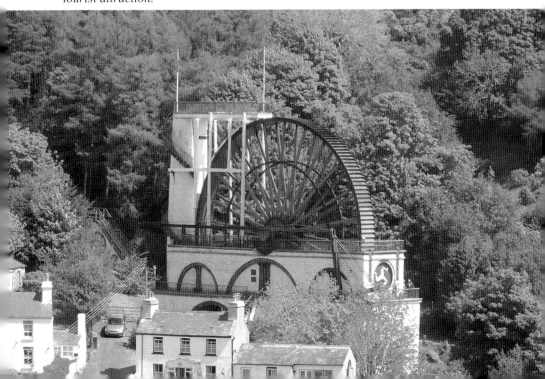

was a visitor attraction, was no longer patronised and lost £95 before the end of the financial year. Lack of confidence in the industry in general, rising costs and the lack of funds to invest in production would cause problems for the mine throughout the war. Yet, while some industries were facing an uncertain future, other industries on the island would find the war very profitable.

The commandeering of the Steam Packet Company vessels was one of the two significant decisions that drastically affected the fortunes of the island. The other was to set up internment camps for enemy aliens. While the former decision brought about much financial distress, the latter helped to generate wealth. The gap between the rich and the poor would widen significantly during the course of the war, as those disadvantaged by one decision were unable to take advantage of the other.

If the lack of vessels made it difficult to cross the Irish Sea, the fear of U-boats and mines was an even greater deterrent. Only those who had urgent or absolutely necessary business would attempt it. Despite the lack of vessels disabling the tourist industry, there was a general feeling of pride that the steamers of the Steam Packet Company, some with Manx names would be flying the flag and going into battle for the homeland. The three passenger vessels that were left all but ceased bringing visitors to the island. Instead, they brought those who had no choice about the crossing: enemy aliens bound for the camps.

Soon after war had been declared, a British Government committee was appointed with the express purpose of dealing with the internment of enemy aliens. Sir William Byrne was chairman of the committee and the decision to use the Isle of Man for an internment camp has been attributed to his memory of Cunningham's Holiday Camp. That memory may very well have saved the island from bankruptcy.

Cunningham's Camp, owned by Joseph Cunningham, had been an innovative concept since it first opened in 1894. It quickly became a serious, and sometimes unwelcome, rival to the boarding house. It was designed for young men and its main attraction was that it was cheap. It could house over 2000 men sleeping under canvas who, despite temperance principles and the need to be in by locking up time, could find plenty of entertainment on site. Tents were cheap to maintain and the large number of guests meant that the huge quantities of food needed could be purchased at good prices. From necessity, the camp

Ballasalla Loyal Manx Association, after, or possibly before duty at the Douglas camp. Courtesy of Manx National Heritage

had modern industrial-sized kitchens capable of preparing hundreds of meals a day, and as the camp was on empty land just outside Douglas, there was the room and flexibility to make alterations. It seemed an ideal location for an internment camp.

There was no consultation over the internment of aliens with the local population and having the enemy on the doorstep was not exactly welcome news. When challenged, the Governor said that all the prisoners were civilians who had been arrested in England and that many of them were of a superior class. There were a number who had English wives, there were many who had never even been to Germany, and all would be guarded by armed soldiers and barbed wire.

On Tuesday, 22 September, the first batch of aliens landed at Douglas. This was only a few days after it had been announced that Cunningham's Holiday Camp would be used to house those interned. On the Monday afternoon it had leaked out that the *Tynwald* was sailing to an unknown destination. The people were quick to associate the secretive departure of the steamer with the transport of prisoners, and prepared to gather the following morning to see this momentous event.

Despite the fine, but bitterly cold, morning and the early hour, several hundred, possibly even a thousand, gathered at the pier to witness the arrival of the captives. Those who had been very early and were close to the disembarkation area were moved at about 5.00 am as the Pier Police closed the gates. Shortly afterwards, a detachment of the Isle of Man Constabulary arrived and they were followed by two detachments of the Isle of Man Volunteers. The disembarkation took about half an hour, from 5.30 am. The prisoners were lined up in a column of threes, guarded at intervals on both sides by the police, who were unarmed, and the Volunteers, who had rifles with bayonets fixed and would act as escort for the march to the detention camp.

If the authorities were concerned that the aliens would receive a hostile reception or that there would be trouble among those who had gathered, they need not have worried. The crowd showed more pity and curiosity than hostility and they even exchanged a few words or a wave of the hand. Just as many locals, anxious to see what the prisoners looked like, had gathered at the pier, there were many others who lived on the route the prisoners would take. They were said to have taken vantage points at windows or on balconies, to watch the spectacle while still in various stages of *deshabille*.

The captives were a mixed group. The *Isle of Man Examiner* described them as a 'motley crew'. Many appeared to be in poor physical condition, although some 'bore themselves in a fashion which indicated military training'. There were plenty who clearly had very limited means. However, wealth or class had been no barrier to internment. Some were noted for their fashionable smart lounge suites or immaculate kid gloves; and one was even rumoured to have had the ability to have had a cheque of seven figures honoured in Britain prior to the war.

Once at the camp, the prisoners found not just barbed wire and armed guards, but tents with straw mattresses, army blankets and food deemed to be 'somewhat better' than that served at the local jail. There was space for physical recreation and they were allowed to wear their own clothes, although they also had to wear a metal disc engraved with an identification number. They were allowed books, and over time started workshops, produced works of art and set up theatrical groups. The whole cost of the camp was to be borne by the British Government.

Just as the prisoners were arriving, the Governor issued the 'rules' that the locals had to abide by when in the vicinity of the camp, and the following was published in various Manx papers:

'His Excellency the Governor has caused the following warning to be issued with regard to the Aliens' Detention Camp:

1. 'This is to give notice that the Camp, commonly known as the "Cunningham Holiday Camp", is now enclosed as a camp for the detention of Enemy Aliens, and will be strictly controlled and guarded.
2. 'No person shall approach or loiter near the precincts of the said camp.
3. 'Any person approaching the precincts of the camp after sundown will be liable to be challenged by the sentries. A person so challenged must immediately halt and await the sentry's permission to proceed. Failure to observe this instruction will involve risk of life to the person concerned.
4. 'No person shall attempt to effect conversation or communicate with an enemy alien under detention, or to convey to or from such an alien any letter, parcel, or other article.
5. 'Any person failing to observe the foregoing directions, or refusing or neglecting to obey the commands of any sentry or other person placed in authority, will be liable to the proper measures and penalties.'

It was not long before someone fell foul of the rules.

On 26 September, Manx artist John Holland, and his son had a photographic appointment in Laxey. John Alexander Holland, being ready before his father, decided to go out for a walk, and with him he took his camera. It was perhaps unfortunate that he happened to live in the vicinity of the camp. In going out for a walk he could not help but pass close by. When he, and his camera, were seen by the sentry, it was decided to have him followed. After his walk he met up with his father but, before the two men could leave for their appointment, the younger man was informed that he was under arrest.

A few days later John Alexander Holland was brought before the police court. He denied taking pictures of the camp, claiming that it would have been madness to do so from the field he was seen in, as there was no view. He also pointed out that if he had wanted to take a picture of the camp he could easily have done so from his own house. Crucially, there had not been any photographs of the camp in the camera. Ultimately the prosecution did not press the charge. It was stated that this was not intended to be a punishment for the defendant, but be a warning to others that the camp was a serious place and any infringement of government rules would be dealt with accordingly. The prosecution said that as there was no photograph of the camp they were prepared to give the defendant the benefit of the doubt. However, rather questionably, they claimed the defendant had been acting most suspiciously. Firstly, they claimed, he had been walking through a field where there was no justification for saying a right of way existed. This was in spite of the fact that it was commonly used. Secondly, they said he did not have any right to loiter around the boundaries of the camp which, considering where he lived, might be a rule difficult to impose.

By late October 1914 there were 2600 prisoners in the Douglas camp, which was just about its limit. However, to relieve congestion at various places of internment in London, a temporary increase was granted to allow 3300 prisoners. Even so, this did not fulfil the needs of the British Government. A deputation was sent, including Sir William Byrne, to determine how suitable the island was for holding larger numbers of aliens. In pouring rain the deputation took a tour of the island, visiting various places and interviewing officials and leaders of public opinion.

Sir William claimed that there were several classes of aliens that required concentration. These ranged from the dangerous, who may have needed a strict military camp, through to the women, children and the elderly who posed no threat, but for their own safety required to be taken into custody. For all classes, Sir William said that the Isle of Man had a distinct advantage as a detention area. The many, empty for the winter, boarding houses were of particular interest, and it would be 'convenient' for the British Government to send large numbers of women and children. Also, there was the space to create concentration camps for those regarded as 'dangerous'.

Sir William was aware that there were disadvantages to having a camp inside or near a town and believed it would be unlikely that there would be any extension permitted in the vicinity of Douglas. He was also convinced that the inhabitants of the island would show their patriotism by rendering service to the Empire and would gladly accept the prisoners sent to them. Indeed, as the British Government would be paying for all the costs associated with the building of a new camp, the feeding and housing of prisoners as well as the guarding of them, the island was going to benefit.

At the same time, W. Ralph Hall Caine, son of the Manx novelist and politician Thomas Hall Caine, was hoping to help out small groups of Belgium refugees. The turning of the island into what he described as 'a vast German prison and hotel' effectively ended his scheme. He decided that it would be unkind to ask the Belgians to live side by side with the Germans. His plan may have failed at the first hurdle, but he held no grudge.

> 'It is a supreme test of our loyalty,' he wrote on the acceptance of internees, 'but as "they also serve who duly stand and wait", so we serve the British cause almost as much by receiving these aliens within our borders as by the slaughter of the enemy-alien on the field of battle.'

Despite the presence of German aliens, a small number of Belgian refugees did come to the island and were very appreciative of the hospitality they received.

Regardless of anyone's feelings about housing a large number of internees on the island, the plan for a new camp went ahead. Knockaloe, just outside Peel, was the place chosen and by the beginning of November work was progressing. Mark Carine was the contractor. He employed about sixty men for the work and sourced materials locally. The original plan was to build twenty-nine houses measuring 150 feet by 30 feet and each capable of accommodating 200 men. There would also be dining halls, offices and officers' quarters. By the end of the war over 20,000 aliens would be housed there, and the building, feeding and upkeep of the camp were significant inputs into the island's economy.

While the camp was being prepared for aliens who would be prisoners, there was some discussion over the other internees who would be 'on parole', residing in hotels and only needed to present themselves for roll call. These were seen as falling into three distinct groups. Firstly, there were the British-born women who were married to enemy aliens, and their British-born families. Secondly, there were wives of internees who hailed from enemy nations themselves, and their families, and finally, there were the well-to-do and elderly enemy

Gate to Knockaloe, thought to be the hospital camp. Courtesy of Manx National Heritage

aliens who had been resident in England for many years and had never displayed dangerous behaviour.

In the House of Keys there were some objections to the plans for those who would not be held in the camps. Whereas the British-born wives would be welcome, it was felt by some, that to have large numbers of Germans and Austrians on the island with no restraint other than the roll call would bring alarm and be resented by the public.

Wives of aliens did visit the island over the course of the war, but the boarding houses were never filled with Germans and Austrians as had been suggested. Baron von Bissing, brother of General Mortiz von Bissing, was in fact the only alien to live outside the camps when he was sent to the island in 1917.

The work for boarding house keepers that could have been provided by housing aliens was an opportunity missed, though few realized it in the early days. Indeed, some refused to have Germans under their roof as it was 'unpatriotic'. Others, however, were soon asking to house aliens to provide them with work. These differences of opinion over the question of the enemy being on the island were not just confined to the boarding house keepers. Across the island there were those advocating that there was no risk to the population from the presence of aliens, that any one of sense could see that it was quite reasonable for the island to accept them and that the venture could be profitable. However, not everyone was of the same mind and the newspapers were always ready to exploit a good story and play on people's fears.

The *Ramsey Courier* waded into the argument by saying that the first batch of prisoners for Knockaloe had been described as a 'double-distilled elixir of rascality'. The *Isle of Man Examiner* made a pointed remark, saying that the second batch of prisoners were 'a decided improvement on their predecessors'. Regardless of anyone's point of view, the relationship between the island and the prisoners, neither of whom had a say in the matter, looked set to be an uncomfortable one.

For the internees, some who regarded themselves as British and many who resented their imprisonment, life was monotonous. It was not long before some displayed symptoms described as 'moroseness, avoidance of others, and an aimless promenading up and down the barbed wire boundary of the compound, like a wild animal in a cage'. It became known as 'barbed wire disease'.

There were several causes of this strange behaviour suggested, but chief among them was boredom. There were attempts to alleviate the boredom, mainly by Quakers, but this was met by public condemnation. For most prisoners there were few opportunities for employment, little privacy, no release date and very limited contact with the outside world, friends or family.

These reasons, along with overcrowding, complaints about the food and poor weather, for which the canvas of the Douglas camp was not suitable, may all have played a part in the riot that occurred at the Douglas camp that autumn.

Trouble started on the evening of 5 November. That day had been particularly wet so after dinner the prisoners refused to return to their tents. Colonel Madoc, who was in charge of the camp, addressed the men and told them firmly that they had no choice; they had to return. With some misgivings, they did, and the incident appeared to have been resolved.

Two weeks later, however, after lunch on 19 November, a second and far more serious incident occurred. A group of prisoners suddenly began throwing chairs, cutlery and crockery, and then they made a charge for the kitchens. At the time only a few sentries were on duty in the dining room. They quickly raised the alarm and were joined by members of the Volunteers and the National Reserve. Greatly outnumbered and being faced with a mob, the soldiers opened fire. Most shots were fired into the air but five prisoners were hit. Four died at the scene, and one died later in hospital.

At the inquest, it was shown that one prisoner, Kurt Faust, had been stirring up trouble over the food. He had been encouraging other prisoners to remove the number tags they were required to wear and saying that there were arms inside the camp. He had also been spreading rumours that 'something awful' was going to happen.

The complaints about the food were not founded and the only genuine complaint that could be verified was about some potatoes. A few weeks earlier worms had been found in them and the potatoes were replaced. However, Colonel Madoc did admit that after a search two revolvers and ammunition were discovered in the possession of prisoners. Also an iron knuckle-duster was found inside a boot in a parcel which censors prevented from reaching its intended recipient.

It took just ten minutes for the jury to come to their unanimous decision. The deaths were caused by justifiable measures forced upon the military by the riotous conduct of the internees. The guards had done their duty and would not face charges of murder. Kurt Faust, however, would be sentenced to five years imprisonment for inciting disaffection.

As the year drew to a close, there was further trouble at the camp, this time testing its administration. Two prisoners were called to a military court both accused of 'acting in a manner prejudicial to the good order of the camp' or, in this case, of communicating with the enemy in invisible ink.

Both Otto Luz and Herman Blass, neither of whom denied the charges, said that they had been encouraged to write secret messages by other prisoners. Otto had been trying to gain information about his two brothers who were fighting in the German army and Herman wanted to complain about how he was being treated and the food. Clearly Herr Blass had not made any serious attempt to evade the censors as he had written in his letter that there was something else written in invisible ink! At least the Manx population could be assured that the censors were doing their job.

Outside the camps the island was preparing for Christmas. Despite the unusual circumstances of war, one of the main questions being debated was not conflict, but temperance. This may seem bizarre to us today, but the movement had a sizable following on the island at the time, and just before Christmas a public meeting was called. At the meeting the Governor was called upon to use his influence to ensure that the Intoxicating Liquor Temporary Restriction Act became operational locally.

For those at the meeting, drink was a serious enemy. English soldiers guarding the camps were a particular problem. They were giving the impression that a soldier's life was one of drink, and they were leading the men of the island who had donned the King's uniform astray. Women, many of whom were suffering loneliness from the absence of their husbands or sons, were also seen as vulnerable to the temptation of liquor. They were drinking more heavily and thereby spending the money intended for their upkeep.

The public meeting denounced the Governor for not having done his duty so far, but felt sure that once he understood that public opinion approved of shorter licensing hours he would do all he could to extend the Act. It would not be the first time the Governor would be regarded as having failed and, unfortunately for Lord Raglan, it certainly wouldn't be the last.

From the beginning of August, 1914 had been a year filled with surprise, turmoil and change. The promise of the season had come to an abrupt halt. Instead, men had left to join various sections of the armed forces, most of the Steam Packet Company vessels had been commandeered and in the place of visitors, thousands of internees had arrived.

When asked by an MHK what effect the internees would have on the season for 1915, the Governor, one of the few people in a position to know that the war was likely to be quite lengthy, replied: 'If the war is over there will be no Germans; if it is not over there will be no visitors.' The ominous undercurrent to his words would prove only too true.

CHAPTER 2

1915
Deepening Conflict

As 1915 dawned there was no immediate end to the conflict in sight. However, there was war work connected to the camps, which provided income. It was also expected that some visitors would return for the season and help ease the financial concerns of the island's most important industry. Unfortunately, this expectation was largely misplaced.

As early as January 1915, German U-boats were seen in the Irish Sea. At the beginning of February, Admiral Hugo von Pohl published a warning in the *Imperial German Gazette* stating that 'all the waters surrounding Great Britain and Ireland, including the whole of the English Channel, are hereby declared to be a war zone'. The Admiral's warning continued to say that, from 18 February, all enemy merchant vessels within the war zone would be destroyed without it always being possible to avoid danger to crew and passengers, and that neutral ships could also be in danger, or be mistaken for enemy ships.

The warning was too late for the first local victims of the U-boat offensive. The SS *Ben Cruachan*, the SS *Linda Blanche* and the SS *Kilcoan* were all sunk on 30 January. The crew on all three ships were given warning and were allowed to evacuate. The crew of the *Kilcoan* were ordered to Douglas, where the harbour master, acting on behalf of the Shipwrecked Mariners' Association, found them lodgings for the night.

Prior to the sinking of the *Kilcoan*, a small steam ship, *Gladys*, had been approached by the U-boat and brought alongside to take the crew. It is likely that the captain of the U-boat had mistaken *Gladys* for a trawler, as no doubt her real cargo, coal for the Douglas Gas Light Company, would have been enough to make her a target as well.

In March the sinking of the SS *Princess Victoria* without warning to the crew showed that submarine warfare was taking a more sinister tone. Captain John Cubbin was from the Isle of Man as were Chief Officer Hugh Kinley and six other members of the crew.

Nevertheless, it was the sinking of the *Bayano* that probably made the greatest impression on the Manx people in early 1915. HMS *Bayano* was not a Manx ship and only three members of the crew hailed from the island. First Class Petty Officers William Gale and John Kelly were reservists from Peel and Second Steward James Atcheson was from Ramsey. All three were lost. However, several other bodies from the wreckage were found, and as they were brought into either Douglas or Ramsey, inquests had to be held.

High Bailiff Gell opened proceedings at Douglas court house on 19 March. During the inquest, three bodies were identified and the cause of death was found to be exposure. Two of the bodies, Leading Seaman James Raymond Geraghty, and First Class Petty Officer Albert Alfred Hellyer, were interred at Douglas.

Despite the fact that these men were not from the island, 'thousands', according to reports, watched the cortege make its way to the cemetery. The White Ensign was placed on the hearses and there was a full military procession. The Isle of Man Volunteers, under Sergeant W. Morgan, were preceded by the Douglas Town Band and were followed by a section of the Loyal Manx

Grave of J.R. Geraghty, who died when the Bayano *was torpedoed, Douglas Cemetry.*

Grave of A.A. Hellyer who died when the Bayano *was torpedoed, Douglas Cemetry.*

Association, a detachment of the National Reserve and officials from the Fire Brigade and Douglas Corporation.

With a respectful slow march and solemn music, the procession made an emotional sight. Two local clergymen conducted the ceremonies and, after final prayers, a volley was discharged over both graves and buglers sounded the Last Post.

At the end of the service, the Reverend Shenton, from St Barnabas's Church, who conducted the service for Petty Officer Hellyer, said that he voiced the feelings of 'this great crowd' when he extended his sympathy to the family of the dead hero. Clearly many on the island did want to express their sympathy and pay their respects.

Few could have failed to recognise that the U-boat menace would mean that it was now highly unlikely that many people would willingly cross the Irish Sea. In any case, the Admiralty had already refused permission for the Steam Packet Company to increase its sailings, something it would need to do to bring the usual seasonal visitors. The island was also plunged into darkness as the Extinction of Lights Order in April brought a blackout, partly intended to hide the island from U-boats.

If there was any hope left for the season, it was completely destroyed with the sinking of the ocean liner *Lusitania*.

The tragedy of the *Lusitania* caused outrage among the civilian population both in England and America. Today we have evidence to suggest that the *Lusitania* was carrying ammunition and therefore, might have been a legitimate target. There have also been suggestions that the British Government hoped for an incident such as this to draw the Americans into the war.

Certainly the British Government lost no time in using the incident for its own propaganda purposes. They had a Lusitania Medal made and put copies for sale on the foreign markets. This fake medal was supposedly to show how Germany had premeditated the attack and how they praised those responsible for the huge loss of civilian life. It was intended to turn opinion against Germany. It is hard to say how effective it was at doing this and it still took another two years before its main aim was realized and America joined the allies.

For the Isle of Man, the *Lusitania* was a story of heroism. German submarine U-20, which had already sunk the *Princess Victoria*, attacked the *Lusitania*, arguably without warning, just off the coast of County Cork.

Just a few miles away, there was a small fishing boat, *Wanderer*, from Peel. Having seen the *Lusitania* go down bow first, it made its way to the scene despite the obvious presence of enemy submarines. *Wanderer* was one of the first rescue boats to arrive and it picked up 160 survivors. Crewman Stanley Ball, son of the skipper, wrote to his mother describing the events of the day:

'The first person we took aboard was a child of two months. We had four or five children aboard and a lot of women. Some of them were naked. I gave a pair of trousers, a waistcoat and an oil-coat away. Some of us have lost a lot, but we expect to get it made up to us. One of the women had her leg broken, another, her arm, and many were very exhausted.'

Among those rescued by the *Wanderer* was Mr D.A. Thomas, a millionaire coal magnate, who gave the crew £20 as a gift. It was also expected that Cunard would remunerate the men for clothing and other items that were given up to help survivors.

The Manchester Manx Society was so impressed by the bravery displayed by the crew that it awarded them medals. These medals were presented by the Governor to the men on the following Tynwald Day. The captain was given a silver one and the rest of the crew were given bronze ones. As the men stepped forward to receive the honour there was much clapping and cheering from the crowd. The people were proud of their local heroes.

Islanders were not just involved in the rescue. There were several Manx residents on board the *Lusitania* on that fateful journey. Seaman James Todd and first class bedroom steward T. Comerford were lucky. Both were saved, but unfortunately the twenty-three year old engineer, W.S. Quarrie, and several others were either missing or confirmed as having perished.

It was the story of Miss Violet James, though, whose letter to her sister brought the tragedy most vividly to life. Miss James was the daughter of a local dentist. She had sailed on the *Lusitania* believing that by travelling via New York she would be safe. Like many other passengers, she was unaware of the late warning the German Embassy had given about how Germany saw *Lusitania* as a legitimate target and that she could fall prey to a U-boat attack.

After being saved, Miss James was taken to Queenstown. Despite her limbs being bruised and swollen from being so long in the water, and despite being 'fagged', as she described herself, she was able to write a few lines from her bed. Of her experience she wrote that she had tried to keep calm and help keep others calm, as well as helping to push the lifeboats off the davits. She suffered a few injuries, but luckily these were only minor and did not impede her survival. It was still too early for her to have recovered from the shock, but she was able to recount her experience and describe how it had strengthened her resolve. To her sister she wrote:

'I tried to get in a lifeboat, but it was too full and the sailor said "No more, lady". The last I remember was facing the captain and second in command and they were facing me. Oh their faces when the water closed over. They put their hands to their faces, poor men. Well down we went and came up. It was nice warm water too. Then I struck out. Thank God I could swim. I have got my life belt with me and will bring it over and you may have it as a souvenir. This is an experience I shall never forget, and I am glad of it. I would kiss the Kaiser's feet now for I know that God will deal with him, and King John's death [a painful one from dysentery in 1216] is nothing to what the Emperor will go through later.'

It is fortunate that her experience did not deter her from sailing again as she had promised to return to Los Angeles within the next month. Of that journey she said: 'We sail under the American flag next, and will make sure of it too'.

If the *Lusitania* sinking had hardened general opinion against the German population, on the island this was made more acute by another incident the day after. Alien prisoners were allowed to leave the camps, under guard, for exercise. In this case they had been allowed out on a picnic, but on their route back to Douglas they were able to see the news placards announcing the loss of the Cunard liner. Their reaction was one of 'jubilation' and hastened the end of their limited freedom to go beyond the wire. In the newspapers this reaction was thoroughly condemned and The *Ramsey Courier* said it should 'make every Manxman's blood boil'. Certainly it did not endear the aliens to the Manx population.

For the boarding house keepers there was now a dilemma. The season could not possibly happen as even the few people brave enough to cross the sea had been put off by the fate of the *Lusitania*. Also, it was now too late for the hoteliers to give notice on their tenancies, as this should have been done in February. Ironically, unknown to prospective tourists and those working in the industry, the transporting of enemy nationals effectively made the Steam Packet Company ships immune to U-boat attack.

Without any income, many were facing penury. In some cases the men had been able to find extra work either through joining up or working at the camps, which gave then an alternative income. Many boarding houses, though, were run by spinsters or widows who had few other options for making a living.

It was not just the lady boarding house keepers who were worried about the situation either. Their landlords often depended on the rents, as did the mortgagees of the properties, and many tradesmen depended on the custom of the boarding houses. The local councils were also suffering as the lack of tourists meant that many of the amenities were not generating an income and so they badly needed the money from rates.

It had been suggested that the 'better-class aliens' could be provided for in the now empty guest houses. However, the idea of having Germans living as 'guests', did not please everyone. Among the boarding house keepers and others who depended on the season, opinion was divided. Some would accept aliens rather than starve; others would not.

In May a letter appeared in the *Isle of Man Examiner* from the proprietor of Garside's Empress Private Hotel. This letter pointed out that the two alien camps were benefitting certain people and why should the idea of housing aliens not benefit more? There had been various solutions suggested, such as billeting of troops, convalescents and Belgium refugees; however, none had succeeded. Therefore a petition was being prepared to send to the Home Secretary asking for aliens to be housed in the island's hotels and guesthouses. It was the opinion of J. Garside that it was work that the lodging-house keepers wanted, not charity or ruin, therefore they should attempt to make this final option a reality.

The women of Douglas who ran boarding houses had already banded together and had formed their own league. They were trying to force the Manx Government to give them either work or compensation as the distress they were in was no fault of their own and there were no viable alternatives. Unlike the seaside towns on the mainland that had fallen into decline, the tourist towns on the island were not near centres of industry where alternative employment could be found.

They had already stated their case to the Governor and they had held several meetings. The resolutions passed at these meetings echoed their wish to have immediate assistance and there were several ways in which this could be done. The billeting of soldiers or convalescents had been discussed as one option, but they could also see arguments for the government relieving them of their tenancies or giving them a significant grant from the accumulated fund.

The League that the lady boarding house keepers of Douglas had set up then set about enlisting the support of the ladies of Ramsey and the other towns. Just prior to the meeting in Ramsey, the British Government announced that it might have to find somewhere to intern the significant number of aliens taken into custody for their own safety following the *Lusitania* sinking.

Were the ladies of Douglas expecting to take Germans? It was a question to which the Ramsey ladies wanted to know the answer. In general, the Douglas ladies were in favour of accepting Germans and petitioning the government for them, as it was better than nothing. In Ramsey some were more vocally against the idea. 'Well, we don't want them', a certain Mrs Jopson said during the course of the meeting. 'We won't have them. We'll all have our throats cut.' Her words may have been somewhat extreme, but they were greeted with applause. Luckily, agreeing to take aliens was not a prerequisite of joining the League and the ladies of Ramsey were free to sign the petition or not, as they chose.

Also in attendance at the meeting was W.T. Crennell, MHK, member for Ramsey. He said that he was pleased to come and meet the ladies and would give whatever help was within his power. There had been a degree of criticism of the government over the position the boarding house keepers now found themselves in. Mr Crennell claimed that it was unfair to accuse the government of inertia as they had appointed a committee to look into the matter. The committee had suggested various measures, including billeting soldiers on the island. However, the British Government had declined to take up the offer; similarly it had decided not to send convalescents. The question of aliens being sent to live in boarding houses was one of which he approved. He recognized that it might become a nuisance to try and censor every letter leaving the island, which would be necessary under such circumstances, but as it was likely that only women and children would live as open prisoners, it would perhaps be desirable to bring them to the island if the alternative was to starve or accept charity. However, he pointed out that only a relatively small number would be wealthy enough to pay their own costs. The rest would be paid for by the British Government, but unfortunately, the payment it was prepared to make would be one or two shillings below what the boarding house keepers would need to keep them.

There had been enquiries into whether alternative employment could be found, but, as Mr Crennell said, while there appeared to have been several options for men, the same could not be said for the women. Shirt making had been mentioned by the Governor but had been criticised, as many felt that this only brought in a few pennies. Mr Crennell believed that criticism of the Governor over his reference to shirt making had been unfair. He had it on authority that even this very small measure had helped some people. It was also hoped that labour bureaus would be set up in the various towns which, working with the labour bureaus in England, would give advice to and assist young women to take up suitable employment across the water.

While he agreed that shirt making might just help out with the cost of living, the problem of paying rent and rates was more difficult to overcome. He hoped that some scheme would be devised, either by loans or other means, to help tide the tenants over the present trouble. Mr Crennell had promised to give his support to the ladies but his message was undoubtedly pessimistic.

The distress of those involved with the visiting industry was well broadcast. There were various reports in the newspapers in England, especially in Manchester and Liverpool, and a comprehensive article about the situation appeared in the *Yorkshire Post*. Often this situation was compared to the increasing wealth of other sections of the community, such as farmers, who were benefitting from increased food prices and custom generated by the need to feed the camps at Douglas and Knockaloe.

Problems for the boarding house keepers would continue for the duration of the conflict but, by 30 June 1915, the question of whether the boarding houses should take aliens had been resolved. In a letter to the Governor, Sir John Simon, Secretary of State for the Home Office, praised the island's patriotism for giving so much help already in terms of aliens and said that it was planned to increase the number of those interned. However, there was no plan to allow aliens to live in boarding houses. Should that position change, and it was found necessary to send a small number over who would be kept under strict supervision, he felt sure the British Government would be able to 'appeal to the

Lord Raglan, Governor of the Isle of Man 1902-1918. Courtesy of Manx National Heritage.

patriotism of the island, to accept the inconvenience which their presence would entail.'

Effectively this closed what was to be the final opportunity for the women of the Douglas boarding houses to make a reasonable living.

Various representations had been made to Lord Raglan, asking for his help. He showed sympathy and generally was very pleasant. However, he ended every meeting by saying he could not help because he did not have the money. Perhaps he was unable to comprehend the island's capacity to generate income, or maybe it was just a refusal to help or attempt to redistribute wealth. Either way, the stubbornness of the man who had been the first to advise boarding house keepers to sell up, was storing up problems for both the less wealthy sections of society and for himself.

For those boarding house keepers who were lucky enough to have Alexander Gill as their landlord there was good news. The self made man had been a builder and by 1914 owned 160 properties in Douglas, mainly on the sea front. He let it be known in the early summer of 1915 that rents for his properties would, for that year and for the rest of the war, be reduced to one third. Whether or not he could afford this reduction, he recognized that it may well be a case of this or nothing and, as he had no wish to cause misery to others, he would not chase debts if even this reduced amount was too much for some to pay.

Finally, that spring, the Manx Government did come up with the 'Loan Scheme to Distressed Boarding House Keepers', which was adopted by Tynwald in June. It might have sounded promising, but many were to be disappointed that this measure fell well short of meeting the needs of those who, through no fault of their own, had fallen on hard times.

This scheme meant that the hoteliers could borrow money on certain, extremely harsh, terms. Their landlords would have to accept one third of the usual rent, the borrower would have to give as security all their furniture and assets, which would became part of a preferential crown debt, and repayment of the loan and five per cent interest had to be made in three years, starting two years after the end of the war.

Many people refused to accept these terms, which meant giving far more security than the loan was worth. They knew that the Governor did not want to impose any direct taxation on his wealthy friends, which was the most obvious and fair way to deal with the situation. They could also see that these terms meant that the assets of the holiday industry would be kept intact for the government once the war ended.

It was estimated that about £50,000 per year would be loaned under the scheme, but as so many felt that the injustice of the terms made the loan unacceptable, by the end of the war only about £12,000 had been borrowed. The loan was not a success and it offered those suffering from war distress nothing. To this background began a fierce political battle that would bring unprecedented scenes to the island in the coming years.

There were other social changes that brought dramatic results as well. The Defence of the Realm Act, or DORA, was particularly good at tripping people up in the wake of the legal changes and increased powers of the authorities that it brought in.

In 1914, John Holland had found to his cost that it was easy to be caught out by new rules that might seem petty, but were meant to be rigidly adhered to. In 1915 more people were to find themselves on the wrong side of law. Arguably, this could have been through nothing more than misjudging the seriousness of the new rules and how they were interpreted.

John James Corlett, a farmer from Andreas, was one such unfortunate. He found himself in court in May 1915 on the charge of making statements 'likely to prejudice the recruiting of his Majesty's Forces'. In April, Mr J.W. Radcliffe, MHK, was making a speech at the Andreas Wesleyan chapel. In front of an audience of about a hundred, including a number of enlisted men, he praised the parish for their contribution of men to the war effort and he made a special mention of several men by name. Afterwards, Farmer Corlett remonstrated with the MHK as he was angry that some of the people who had been named in pride were, in his opinion, shirkers and lazy. In front of a crowded court, he maintained his reference was to their conduct while working in the locality prior to the war. He withdrew his remarks that he had made in the heat of the moment and apologized. However, the argument over whether his remarks would prejudice recruiting caught the imagination of the time and a heavy fine was handed down.

In June, a far more sensational case was brought before a court at Castle Rushen. Ambrose Qualtrough, MHK, was accused of spreading false reports and failing to give information to the Competent Military Authority, when requested in writing, as to who his informants were.

Ambrose Qualtrough was a man of reformist sympathies and, certainly in some quarters, he was popular. However, he frequently found himself on a collision course with a number of his political colleagues including the Governor. It was perhaps unfortunate then, that the Governor, as the Competent Military Authority on the island, would be the very person he was in trouble with.

Ambrose Qualtrough, MHK. Courtesy of Manx National Heritage.

The problems for Mr Qualtrough began on 28 May. He had delivered some beef from his shop in Port Erin to the store house at Chicken Rock. At the store house there were several sailors, one of whom said that the Germans from the Douglas camp had escaped. Mr Qualtrough's reaction was to leave immediately and try to find out if what the sailor had said was true. As he returned to Port Erin he met a gentleman he knew, Mr Capern, a local JP. He asked the JP if he had heard the rumour about the camp. He then telephoned the Government Secretary, Bertram Sargeaunt, believing Mr Sargeaunt would be the one person who could definitely confirm or deny it. Of course, Mr Sargeaunt, who was well aware that the Germans had not escaped, was amused by Mr Qualtrough's question and asked who had told Mr Qualtrough such a story.

Mr Qualtrough refused to give the name of the sailor as it might mean that the sailor would lose his job. Mr Qualtrough's actions may have been very well-meaning, but as he would not give the name of his informant the Governor issued an order.

> 'I, being a Competent Military Authority, do hereby require you, AMBROSE QUALTROUGH, of PORT ERIN, forthwith to furnish to me in writing, the name, address and description of the person or persons who informed you to the effect that four thousand aliens had escaped from the Douglas Aliens Camp.'

The instruction to provide an immediate answer seems very clear, but Mr Qualtrough's reply to the policeman who had delivered the order was that he would respond within a week. He felt that this was sufficient. The order had been served on a Saturday afternoon when Mr Qualtrough was working in his shop. He did not believe that he could be expected to answer at such a time, or that he could be expected to answer the next day, which was a Sunday.

However, the authorities, who had used the word 'forthwith' in the order, did not agree. As no answer appeared to be forthcoming, a summons was issued on the Tuesday. The summons at least generated a reply. On the Wednesday, Mr Qualtrough wrote to the Governor explaining that he was unable to give him a name as the sailors who were around the stores at Chicken Rock were all strangers.

Considering Mr Qualtrough had so little information, it seems that his actions were foolhardy to say the least. Was he being obstructive on purpose or did he genuinely believe he was protecting the unknown sailors while grossly underestimating the seriousness of DORA regulations? Equally we could question whether the authorities rather over-reacted to something that was relatively trivial, or whether they took the opportunity to discredit a difficult MHK.

Fines of £5 for spreading false stories and £5 for refusing to comply with the request to name the informant were handed down. The defendant decided he would not pay and chose instead to go to prison for two weeks. When interviewed afterwards, he said that he had always been hounded for his reformist views and that as justice on the island was impossible because of the 'rule of one man', that being the Governor, he knew he would be fined.

Certainly his beliefs would not be popular in some sections of the local population. He believed that there should be some form of income tax which would, by its nature, be levied on the wealthy. Many of the officials of the island would therefore have to pay this tax. He even went so far as to say that the island should be annexed by England and become part of Lancashire. This would enable the people to access certain financial benefits such as old age pensions and war distress relief, but certain appointed officials would then lose their roles and the income that came with it. However, there is no doubt that he failed to comply with a direct order and that was the main reason he was prosecuted. If he had answered the Governor's questions immediately, his so-called spreading of false reports may well have been overlooked. It seems he sacrificed himself on a matter of principle, but achieved very little towards his aim of relieving the suffering of the Manx people and 'give them freedom', as he called it. The *Isle of Man Examiner* expressed very plainly the difficulties Mr Qualtrough brought upon himself.

> 'It is very unfortunate that so well-meaning a gentleman as Mr Ambrose Qualtrough, HK, should constantly look for trouble for himself, and it is more unfortunate still that he should so frequently succeed in the search.'

Ambrose Qualtrough set himself up as a champion of the people, but his success at the ballot box had not translated into positive action. Thankfully for the people though, there were others who were more successful in this respect. In 1916 it would be the reformer and journalist Samuel Norris who would take his place as the foremost people's champion; but in 1915, the mantle fell to a gentleman who had no political motivation whatsoever.

Charles Copeland-Smith was a Wesleyan minister and though not native to the island, he soon made a name for himself as the chairman

Reverend Copeland-Smith who instigated the Manx Industries Association.
Courtesy of Manx National Heritage.

of the Douglas section of the Manx Temperance Federation. He was
shrewd enough to recognise that the war would have an adverse effect
on the finances of the island and that this would hit the women of
Douglas the hardest. As early as September 1914 he had written to the
editor of *Mona's Herald* to call upon the government to announce plans
for work over the winter to help. He also had the foresight to realise
that whatever was to be done had to be done quickly before many

sources of income were cut off and, mostly importantly, before the situation became so bad that it became necessary to make emergency plans in a panic.

In early 1915, Copeland-Smith and the committee of the Douglas section of the Temperance Federation came up with the idea of providing a home for the soldiers billeted on the island. It would be somewhere for them to meet up, buy refreshments (non-alcoholic, of course) and spend some recreational time. By April this small but helpful measure had been put in place and the Governor formally opened the home. Lord Raglan was also generous enough to loan a billiard table for use in one of the recreation rooms.

However, Copeland-Smith intended to make a much bigger social contribution to the people and this was to come through a commercial venture: the Manx Industries Association. Having set up similar projects in Soho and Birmingham, Copeland-Smith decided to use his skills and experience to bring employment to the people of the island who desperately needed it.

Gathering about himself some of the most influential business men, and fostering their support, he embarked upon a mission to revive the old Manx knitting industry. Manx wool had traditionally been used to clothe fishermen and made garments of high enough quality to withstand weather and heavy usage. With this in mind, it seemed obvious to make socks and sell them to soldiers. With the help of selling through the Methodist network, a market was created big enough to support a factory, which opened at the beginning of July. By mid August seventy women were employed and there was a substantial waiting list of applicants for jobs. For many on the waiting list it would not be long before they were employed, as Copeland-Smith procured a government contract in addition to the private trade.

The 100,000 pairs of socks that were ordered by London would mean that another hundred women would be taken on over the winter months. With the flexibility to use his own pattern and confidence in the high quality of the wool spun on the island, Copeland-Smith made an enormous success of his factory. True to the philanthropic beliefs of those behind the venture, the Manx Industries Association never paid a dividend, preferring instead to put profits back into the business. The aim of the project was not to make money but to alleviate financial distress and prevent it from becoming a disaster.

Of all the various deputations that had visited London, and of all the schemes that had been discussed to try and help the situation that Douglas and other parts of the island faced, the Manx Industries Association was the only one that succeeded. Copeland-Smith was personally responsible for much of the scheme's success. His personal involvement was so extensive that, with the blessing of the Douglas Wesleyan Methodist Circuit, the popular preacher had to be relieved of some of his ministerial duties.

Certainly his achievement was much appreciated. Ambrose Qualtrough, whose own attempts to 'help' people had included a futile stay in prison, suggested that one way to solve the island's problems would be to appoint Copeland-Smith as Governor. Even Queen Alexandra wrote a letter praising the business and placing a large order of socks, no doubt destined for troops fighting in her son's name.

As the situation at the front became more serious, and it was obvious that the conflict was greater in scale and was going to be longer lasting than anyone had thought, the situation at home had also become more serious.

More and more people were facing financial hardships and so the divisions that had always been there, between the wealthy and the poor, were becoming more pronounced. From these difficulties the personalities of the war came to prominence as did the conflict between them.

The Governor, a well-known conservative and anti-reformist, had shown himself unable, or unwilling, to help those suffering war distress. His refusal to acknowledge that they even had an argument implied a complete lack of sympathy with, or understanding of the plight of, the working classes. For him, the war was a convenient excuse to hold up any reform measures that would challenge the power that he enjoyed.

This was in stark contrast to the work of Copeland-Smith, and would make Lord Raglan more unpopular with reformists who, in turn, became more dedicated to their cause. Chief among the Governor's reformist adversaries would be Samuel Norris. He had been involved with the reform movement from its beginnings in 1903, but when he decided to help the boarding house keepers in December 1915, he took the fight to a whole new level, although he probably did not realise it at the time.

Before the war there had been many recommendations for reform made by a British Government committee, but very little had come of it. The events of 1915 meant that far more ordinary people now became interested in both the deeds and attitude of the Governor and the general government of the island. The will for reform had picked up greater momentum. The dire situation that many were facing would shape not only people's views but much of what was to come in 1916 and beyond.

CHAPTER 3

1916
Realization

At the beginning of 1916 few would have predicted that it would be a year of such agitation, or that the stalemate at home would be, in its way, as bad as the stalemate at the front.

The year opened quietly. There were a few stories from the camps, but nothing out of the ordinary. There had been a minor fight ending in charges of common assault and petty theft from the camp stores. This was probably nothing worse than what could be expected from forcing a large number of people to live together as prisoners. Far more serious, however, was the escape of four internees from Knockaloe.

As soon as the escape was discovered the descriptions of the four men: Richard Karlsen, George Sudmann, Julian Hoffman and Robert Clauss, were circulated and a thorough search was conducted.

As the four men were sailors it was believed, correctly as it turned out, that they would try to take a boat to escape from the island.

After two nights in the open, the four men tried to take the yacht *Genesta*, belonging to a Mr Wilson of Peel, from Peel harbour. Unfortunately for the escapees, two local fishermen saw that *Genesta* was adrift and alerted the authorities.

With the Isle of Man Volunteers armed on the quayside and the police, sailors and a member of the Volunteers in another boat, the aliens were surrounded and quickly surrendered. From the supplies and equipment they had with them, it could be seen that this was no opportunistic escape, but something that had been carefully planned and with the ultimate goal of reaching Norway.

The story of the capture made a sensational news item. There had been escapes before. Sudmann had already spent time in prison for a previous escape attempt, but this time the preparation that must have been involved raised questions. How had the men managed to gather together the provisions and equipment, including wire cutters, charts and a compass, which would be needed for such an arduous journey? As the four men faced a court martial charged with escaping and with the theft of the boat, for which they were found guilty, questions were raised in the Keys about how the camps were run.

The Keys, however, had another, more important, matter to discuss in the early months of 1916, and that was conscription. Not confined to just the politicians, conscription would also be debated in public and become part of the argument for social and political reform.

In January 1916 *Mona's Herald* published an article entitled 'The Real Slackers'. The article, neither for nor against conscription, posed an important question that would continue to re-surface in the minds of many. If men were to be conscripted into the army, to help the whole community, 'what about those shy gentlemen with large incomes who will not do their part by contributing a just share of their incomes to the revenue?'

Direct taxation, such as income tax or land-based tax, of course, was not liked by many in power as the burden of paying it would fall on them and their wealthy friends. So far the wealthy had been protected. However, the call for this type of taxation, although not new, would grow in volume during 1916. With so many falling into war distress while others were profiting, the injustice of the financial divide was acutely felt. Many believed that they had suffered enough and did not want the extra burden of conscription.

Just because conscription was to become law in England, it did not automatically mean that it would be extended to the island. In fact, the Keys passed a resolution that compulsory service should not be extended to the island without the previous consent of Tynwald being obtained.

There were several arguments against conscription both inside and outside the House. The island had already sent a good number of men off to fight as volunteers and some felt that as the British Government had taken away the island's ability to try and keep the season going by commandeering the Steam Packet vessels, perhaps enough had already been sacrificed.

Others were worried about the effect on agriculture. Most of the farms were significantly understaffed as it was and to take away the rest of the workforce in such a crucial industry could spell disaster. It would not be to just the island's detriment either, as the farms were exporting large quantities of produce to England.

To some it was merely a question of home rule and the principle that the island should not be told what to do by London.

Other people had genuine concerns about forcing some men to join up, especially if those men were the main provider of a household or the main carer of children or other dependent relatives. Army pay may be less than income already being earned and, without old age pensions or other social care on the island at the time, what would happen to their dependants should these men be killed or seriously injured?

The issue was seen to be so contentious that when a public meeting was held in Peel there had been special arrangements made should there be a disturbance and extra police had been drafted in from Douglas.

However, despite the large crowd, there had been no need to worry. There was no disturbance and the resolution of the meeting was carried without dissent. The resolution itself was not just a vote for or against conscription. Intended to be passed onto the Prime Minister, it pointed out how conscription would adversely affect the poorer inhabitants of the island, who had already made great sacrifices for the war and that no such measure should be placed on the island 'until such a time as personal and real estate is made subject to the same forms of direct taxation as in the other parts of the British Isles'.

Despite all the arguments, when it came to a vote in Tynwald it was unanimously decided to extend conscription to the island. It would be a slur on the island not to adopt the Act and they would be seen as poor allies. However, the legislature's decision to send other people to fight was one that was going to be made by them, not London.

The Governor, who enjoyed the power he had, had even taken steps to ensure that the island was not included in the original Act. In his speech before Tynwald voted, he said that the number of conscripts from the island would be relatively few and he praised the island for all the support and sacrifices already made towards the war. Despite this, he was a military man first and foremost. He approved of conscription, he believed that Tynwald would agree to extend it to the island; and no doubt he was proud to preside over a legislature that voted for such a patriotic measure.

A few months later, in May 1916, the Military Service Act was extended to include married men. Although this also passed the vote, there was far more opposition to it. Again much of the argument centred on what would happen to the farms if all the men were taken. Unlike in England, where the training camps were, the island would not be able to 'borrow' men for a few weeks to collect the harvest.

As well as the farms there were other businesses that were run by men and, in the eyes of the men of the time, could not possibly be left to women. As Mr Kermode MHK, said 'if the few married men of military age left in Peel were taken, the town would be deprived of its most active and useful citizens.' There were also questions about how worthwhile it would be to try and take married men. There were so few men left that those who were would almost certainly be exempt at a tribunal, therefore making the whole thing a waste of everybody's time. When it came to a vote in Tynwald, the same argument as before won the day. The island would look unpatriotic if it voted against the measure. It was not worth the risk.

With conscription came various applications for exemptions. There was some sympathy for men who might be the main breadwinner or carer for a family, but few permanent exemptions were granted.

Conscription also brought to notice the conscientious objector. There were a small number of objectors on the island and some, like Harold Lilley, did gain some respect for their views. However, the most notable objector, Elijah Oliver, became more a figure of fun as his behaviour bordered, at times, on the eccentric.

Elijah was an insurance agent, a clerk to the school board of Lonan and a well-known Methodist lay preacher. No doubt religion played a large part in his moral standpoint. He had been ordered to report to the Douglas Recruiting Office on 10 June. As a male, a British subject, and between the ages of 18 and 41 he fulfilled all the required criteria for conscription. He claimed exemption on the grounds of objection and had been ordered to a non-combatant role. He then lost an appeal against the non-combatant order. When he was brought in front of High Bailiff Gell he asked for remand for a week to prepare his defence. He wanted a copy of the Isle of Man Constitution, to ascertain whether orders issued under the Military Service Act were in accordance with it. He also requested copies of the Reserve Forces Act 1882, the Isle of Man (War Legislation) Act and The Military Service (Isle of Man) Act.

The stiff reply from the High Bailiff was that there had been plenty of time to do this already. It looked as if Elijah's fate was sealed and he seems to have been aware of it. He had already said in front of the Bailiff that he recognized that the court was concerned with matters of law and could not be expected to deal with matters of conscience. He was charged as a deserter and fined 40s. He was also to be sent to his regimental headquarters to fulfil a non-combatant role. After spending a night in the island's prison, he still refused to go and join his assignment. He would only go with his escort if they were to remove him physically, something which was normally reserved for the most difficult of criminals.

The next morning a small crowd gathered at the Victoria Pier. They were there to wave off the boat, but they also witnessed a most unusual sight. A small group of soldiers were wheeling a hand cart upon which a man lay strapped to a stretcher. At the top of the steps leading to the gangway he was unstrapped, but as he still refused to go down the gangway he was lifted on the stretcher and carried on board. Once on deck he did stand and waved a white handkerchief at the crowd as the boat left. The crowd knew who Elijah was, and why he was being treated so. Most of those there seemed to look upon the incident with contemptuous amusement rather than with hostility. However, some women, who were waving soldiers off, were said to have shouted sarcastically 'thou shalt not kill' and 'coward'.

Elijah was sent to trial in north Wales on 30 June. Again he conducted his own defence, citing the fact that he was a citizen of the Isle of Man and therefore not bound by the Military Service Act under which his call up papers had been issued. He admitted he was an objector, but that did not absolve the authorities from issuing papers in the correct way.

Unsurprisingly, his defence failed and he was sent to prison. Back in the Isle of Man some were disappointed by what had happened and blamed the authorities for allowing the British Government to interfere with home rule. However, Elijah's behaviour had appeared at times to be childish and his arguments ridiculous. As a result, not all people were as sympathetic towards him. As an article in the *Isle of Man Examiner* said, 'I can conceive that were he a militarist instead of an objector, he would be as ruthless in his bigotry as he is now in the inconvenience he causes to men who, not of the same turn of mind as himself, are but doing their duty.'

While all this was going on, the boarding house keepers and others that depended on the tourism industry were facing another potentially disastrous season. Despite the fact that they knew that Lord Raglan had said, 'never, so long as I am Governor, will I give any relief of rates', they did not give up their fight. They wanted fair rates levied in view of the fact that they had no means to make any income rather than rates levied on the pre-war value of their properties. They wanted grants, not loans, to help relieve them of the rates owing for 1915 and they wanted the ability to use the accumulated fund. The arguments they put forward were strong ones and they knew that the money was available.

In December 1915, Samuel Norris played a crucial part in strengthening the group. He had called two public meetings and here he had brought together the landladies and others who were suffering war distress. At Norris's instigation they agreed to the Passive Resistance Pledge against the payment of unjust rates, and together they formed The Isle of Man War Rights Union. They were now focused on positive action.

In September 1915 the Governor left the island for a period of sick leave. By the spring of 1916 he had still not returned, and even though he probably was genuinely ill, his absence was criticized. In the absence of the Governor, the executive of the War Rights Union met with his deputy, Thomas Kneen. Mr Kneen, although a pleasant man according to Norris, was a strong supporter of the Governor. He had held various posts on the Legislative Council and probably owed his appointment to those posts and the income that came with them to Lord Raglan. He also knew that if he were to give in to the demands of the War Rights Union he would have to increase taxes, and it was highly likely that the British Government would expect those taxes to be on income. Like anyone suddenly faced with higher taxes to pay he did not approve of the idea.

After several meetings and even a public demonstration outside the legislative buildings, it seemed that the War Rights Union would never

Samuel Norris, the island's leading reformer of the period. Courtesy of Manx National Heritage.

be able to achieve anything. The Governor had been adamant that the money was not there to help them, even though it quite obviously was. The accumulated fund was in a very healthy state, but for the British

The Wedding Cake, originally the Bank of Mona and home to the House of Keys since the 1870s.

Government to allow the money to be used it would require the funds to be replenished. Income tax, to which the Manx Government would never agree, was the most obvious way to do this.

The MHKs for Douglas, although expected to support the people of the town, owed various appointments and contracts to the Governor and so were unlikely to vote against him. Even if they had dared, or wanted, to support the idea of income tax, they would almost certainly have been outvoted by the country members, who were more numerous and whose constituencies would have borne the main burden of the tax.

Only the Douglas Town Council, which had already sent a deputation to London on the matter, had shown any active sympathy for the measures requested by the Union. The answer from London had effectively said that the money was there and it could be used, but the island was responsible for ensuring that any funds used were replenished.

In despair, the War Rights Union called another meeting to pass two very important resolutions. The main resolution of the meeting, to call for the intervention of the Home Secretary, was in the hands of a Mrs Poulter. She spoke eloquently and at some length. Even a hostile audience would have had difficulty in not seeing the logic in her arguments. 'What to me,' she said 'has been unexplainable throughout has been the unsympathetic and almost antagonistic attitude of many of our own officials towards us. If the whole disaster had been the result of some act of stupendous folly on our part, we could hardly have received worse treatment.' Later in her speech she gave a mild, but poignant, rebuke to the official inertia the Union had received.

> 'The centre around which so much trouble moves is, of course, taxation. Our officials seem prepared to tax tea, tobacco, beer – anything, in fact, but themselves. They have buttoned up their pockets tightly, and they do not mean to open them to any form of taxation until they are compelled.'

These words would prove to be accurate.

The meeting agreed to the resolution without dissent and a second resolution was then put forward by Samuel Norris. This second resolution would be without precedent.

As secretary of the Union, Mr Norris had called the meeting and invited the five MHKs for Douglas. One of the MHKs had only been elected a few weeks previously so, as it was believed that he supported the Union to a certain degree, little pressure was put on him. As for the other four, they were expected to attend and explain their actions, or lack of, as the case might be. Unfortunately one never responded, one had flu, another did not think anything useful could come from the meeting and the fourth refused to attend any meeting where it had been made public that he would speak before he knew about it. In actual fact, when Norris advertised the meeting he had not said that the MHKs would speak, only that they would be invited to do so.

'Why were they really absent?' Norris asked in his speech. He concluded it was because they were ashamed of their neglect and betrayal of the people of Douglas, and that instead of being servants of the people they were servants of the governor and government.

For these reasons, Norris presented a motion of no confidence in the four members for Douglas. 'This meeting of the electors of Douglas expresses its grave disappointment of the past services of, and its entire want of confidence in, Messrs Carine, Garside, Moughtin and Clucas, as members of the House of Keys, and calls upon them to resign their seats forthwith.'

The vote of no confidence was carried and it was left to Norris to communicate it. How much notice the MHKs in question would take of the resolution was another matter. Elections had effectively been suspended for the duration and the resolution was only passed by between 1000 and 2000 people, depending on which newspaper you believe, whereas the population of Douglas was about 20,000. For similar reasons, and the fact that they had more important things to deal with, the *Isle of Man Examiner* argued that a commission from the Home Office to inquire into the situation in Douglas would be unlikely.

Indeed the *Examiner* would prove to be correct. When the letter from the Home Secretary was received informing the Union of his decision that a commission would be of little use, the Union agreed to accept the argument. However, their acquiescence may have been prompted by another letter sent to the Governor a few days previously. This letter had refused a Bill carried in Tynwald repealing the right of re-assessment and imposing loans for rates on empty and depreciated properties. Keeping the right of re-assessment at war-time value for rates was a small victory.

The letter demonstrated quite clearly the view of the Home Secretary. He could see that while the towns were suffering, the country areas, either through the agricultural conditions of the time or British Government expenditure for the camps, were growing rich. The latter should help the former with taxation imposed to replenish the accumulated fund. The argument that the money was there, it could be used as long as it was replaced and it should be replaced by direct taxation was about to begin yet another cycle.

The Union might have failed in being granted an independent commission, but they were seeing a few small steps towards victory.

Having approached the Home Office directly, they were showing their first actions towards being a political, rather than just financial movement.

Soon after the Home Office's communications with the island there was talk in Tynwald of a 'Land Tax' and other measures. What actually happened was an increase in tea duty, which alone would be expected to bring in about £9000 from tea consumption in the two camps, and would be paid by the British Government. They also passed a Relief of Rates Bill, which kept the pre-war valuation but paid the rates by a grant for one third, a loan to the local authorities for one third, and one third to be paid by the tenant.

It was also decided that the full rates of £36,000 for 1915 should be asked for, or as Samuel Norris put it in his memoirs, 'they decided to extort the £36,000 admittedly unjust and illegal rates for 1915-16 from the boarding house keepers and business tenants, as if these people had had a prosperous season.'

Samuel Norris called this action by the Manx Government 'their culminating folly', and it certainly gave further impetus to the War Rights Union. They agreed that should the Manx Government enforce their decision on the payment of rates that the Union would carry out its Passive Resistance Pledge.

By June, the government's accounts for the year ended 31 March 1916 were available. The Governor had predicted a deficit of £26,000 but instead there was a surplus of £18,000. Total revenue had increased by £30,000, all from customs duties on food, drink and tobacco, which had been paid largely by the working classes and British Government on behalf of the aliens. This incensed a large number of people and another public meeting was called by the War Rights Union for 26 June. This was to be another turning point in the campaign. Within a few days of this meeting the character of the War Rights Union changed from a union trying to address a single issue to a full blown political movement. The War Rights Union, under the same leadership, became the Redress, Retrenchment and Reform Campaign, with its own published 'Manifesto to the Manx People'.

They had already asked for the resignation of certain members of the Keys and now they asked for the resignation of the Governor. Lord Raglan may have had his own reasons for doing so, but by predicting a deficit of £26,000 when it should have been obvious that there would be a surplus, and by his inability to provide realistic financial support to the island's main industry, he was seen as financially inept. In his place the Union wanted a strong Governor who understood finance and who would have some sympathy with the people. They also wanted part of the Governor's salary returned as he had been absent for nearly nine months.

After a public demonstration and a march to the House of Keys, these resolutions were presented to the Speaker. As the resolutions were handed over there were some bitter exchanges between some of the members of the Keys and the members of the deputation. The movement that had called for income tax and the removal of the Governor was regarded with complete contempt by some MHKs, especially those from the country.

It might have been expected that the main business of the day would be the discussion of the resolutions of the War Rights Union. Instead, the main news from Tynwald was that the Governor, Lord Raglan, was to return to the island to resume his duties. On 28 June a second public

Inside the House of Keys today.

meeting was called by the Union to express disappointment in the legislature; and to resolve that they would put their requests forward, by memorial, at the Tynwald Day ceremony. By doing this they would be exercising their ancient, but rarely used, rights.

The campaign leaders also counselled their supporters to stay away from the pier when the Governor arrived. It was anticipated that there could be some ugly scenes and the campaign did not want to be tarnished or leave itself open to criticism.

As it became known that a memorial was to be presented on Tynwald Day, there were some clumsy attempts to keep the campaign members away from the ceremony. This mostly involved visitors, or 'friends', advising them to stay away. This advice was not taken and instead, in the early morning of 5 July three horse-drawn carts, holding about ten people each, took position close to Tynwald Hill. These carts gave the campaign members platforms from which to display placards stating the wishes of the movement. 'WE WANT A NEW GOVERNOR, TAXATION OF WEALTH, NO FOOD TAXES, REVENUE FROM THE CAMPS FOR WAR DISTRESS.'

These placards could be seen from every part of the surrounding grounds, and as the crowds gathered, 5000 copies of the Memorial were circulated. Many people there were in support of the demonstration. After the church service that always precedes the Tynwald Hill ceremony, the church doors were opened for the officials to make their procession to the hill. As they began along the path there was a hostile demonstration, with the Governor being greeted with cries of 'resign' and chants of 'no food taxes', 'old age pensions' and 'redress, retrenchment and reform'. The chants and booing grew in intensity as the procession made its way and would have left the legislature in little doubt of the public feelings towards them.

Silence reigned to allow the ceremony to take place according to custom, but once the Memorial had been presented with a great cheer from the crowd and the ceremony concluded, the procession back to the church began. It was during this procession, again accompanied with much jeering from the crowd, that a small missile, which turned out to be nothing more than a sod of grass, hit the Governor on the hand. Lord Raglan barely noticed, but the 'sodding of the Governor' became a sensational headline in both the local and English press. It was now well known that the Governor of the Isle of Man was

Tynwald Hill at St John's where the Tynwald Day ceremony is still held, showing the path Lord Raglan and the legislature would have used while being jeered in 1916.

St John's church and the walkway to Tynwald Hill.

unpopular. Shortly afterwards, Lady Raglan made an unprecedented move of her own. She announced that she was withdrawing her support from all public works and charitable events owing to the attacks on her husband.

When the organizers of the demonstration at Tynwald Hill arrived home that night, they found summonses to appear in the High Court for non-payment of the rates for 1915. They also found out that the Memorial had not been read in the church as it should have been as it 'contained expressions which were not respectful, decorous, nor was it temperate of language'. In short, the petition was refused without discussion and the authorities were doing everything in their power to crush the political agitation.

When the Reform Campaign members faced court for the non-payment of rates, it was proved under cross examination that they were the only ones prosecuted, although they were not the only ones who owed rates. Some were offered ways to pay but refused, as they were determined that the only way the money was going to be raised was through the sale of their belongings, where they would invoke the Passive Resistance Pledge. They knew that they were being singled out because of their political actions, but refused to be intimidated.

In fact the committee now took it upon themselves to address MPs in England and keep the Home Office aware of developments. To their astonishment they found they had significant support. They were particularly encouraged when, at their request, a Home Office instruction was sent to the local authorities stating that no dependent of a soldier or sailor on active service should have household goods seized for payment of rents or rates.

By October it had been decided that the government would recoup unpaid rates by seizure of goods, regardless of the value of those goods in relation to the amount owed. One person had a piano taken worth £50 while only owing £10.

On 2 October, and also on 3 October, several members of the Redress, Retrenchment and Reform Campaign Committee, including Samuel Norris, were called upon and had various belongings taken. At the time there was about £10,000 outstanding in rates, including money owed by town councillors and other officials, against whom no action was taken.

Unfortunately for Samuel Norris, not only was he secretary of the campaign with his name published on letters and notices, but he had been a journalist. As a journalist he had been present at government sittings and was familiar with proceedings and on speaking terms with many in the legislature. He was well known and seen as the leader of the movement. Worse than that, his landlord just happened to be a judge in the Manx High Court. Little wonder that he was the primary target.

As the coroner's van moved on from house to house collecting goods, a crowd of people followed, drawing attention to what was happening. No one prevented the coroner's men from entering premises and Samuel Norris even encouraged one lady to open her doors as the coroner's men were only doing their duty as the instruments of the law, not the lawmakers.

The goods were sold a few days later without the auctions being advertised. According to Norris's memoirs it was a legal requirement to announce such sales and was another of the legal irregularities on the part of the Manx Government to which the movement was becoming accustomed. Therefore, Norris took matters into his own hands. He printed a flyer announcing the sale and asked people to attend, not to buy, but to refuse to do so and to speak out or jeer at those who did, or at anything else they disagreed with. He was asking people to exercise their right to free speech.

The sale took place at 11.00 am on 6 October. Six hundred people crowded into a hall that usually accommodated only half that number and, before the auction began, and with the coroner's permission, several speeches were made. The speeches informed the audience of the events leading up to the sale and how the speakers were not there as law breakers but as political agitators forced into their position by unjust laws on the island.

Whether the people present were moved by the speeches made, or whether they were general supporters of the movement is unknown, but as the sale proceeded it disintegrated into a farce with uproar and cat-calling directed against those who bid and the authorities who brought the sale about. Ultimately the sale failed, having only raised a few shillings.

The Committee was content with the events of the day and was satisfied with the success that they had so far achieved. They were supported by many residents on the Island, by various MPs in England

and they also had valuable allies in the English press. Criticisms of the Governor in the English press could hardly have been pleasing to him and no doubt Samuel Norris, with his press connections, was seen yet again as a chief culprit.

Significantly, an article appeared in the *Isle of Man Times* on 16 October. It stated that a circular had been sent by the Redress, Retrenchment and Reform Campaign to all MPs explaining that a petition was to come before the House of Commons that week. The petition asked for the resignation of Lord Raglan and for the reform of the Manx Government. The petition had about 6000 signatures which, when taking into account all the wealthy people who would be against direct taxation, and all the people who owed their positions, either directly or indirectly, such as at the camps, to the Governor, it amounted to most of the free adult population of the island.

This may or may not have been the first the Governor knew of the petition, but later that day he signed an order to bring Samuel Norris and eight others before him in the Manx High Court. The charge was for contempt of court for 'wilfully and maliciously' preventing the coroner from carrying out the sale of goods in lieu of rates.

Conducting his own defence, Samuel Norris firstly questioned the lack of political bias in the court. Three members of the bench were part of the legislature whose failings had brought about the political agitation he was involved in, and as such they could not give him a fair hearing. He claimed that he had done nothing wrong but had used his right to free speech in asking people not to buy at the auctions – he had even encouraged people to be co-operative during the seizure of goods. He was given the opportunity to apologize and promise not to interfere with sales in the future. Effectively he had apologized for anything that he might have done that could be illegal, but to refuse to interfere with future sales was an attack on his right to free speech that Norris would not accept.

By his own admission, Norris, under the stress of the court case did not speak as effectively and eloquently as he would normally. He was agitated and the bench claimed that he had not given sufficient apology. What they had really wanted was his promise not to prevent further sales, but they had not anticipated that Norris would stand up for his rights so strongly. In a turn of events that probably not even the bench were expecting, they had backed themselves into a corner and had to send Norris to prison. Possibly because they had not been prepared for this, no length of sentence was stipulated.

The authorities had got their man, but at a price. The resolve of the Redress, Retrenchment and Reform Campaign was strengthened and, as the Governor left the court he was heckled for his decision. The authorities had wanted Samuel Norris, as leader of the movement, to be chastened and to curb the actions of the movement. Instead they made Norris a martyr.

Of the others brought before the court that day, two were acquitted, one was deemed too ill, and the other five were fined £1 and ordered to jail if the fine was not paid within a week. As they all felt that the fine was unjust, none of them paid it, and none of them were ever pressed for it or sent to prison.

Within days of Samuel Norris being committed, several articles appeared in both local and English papers condemning the treatment he had received. Also, friends and supporters quickly rallied and sent food to the prison, which as a civil rather than criminal prisoner Norris was entitled to. Two friends from the campaign were able to visit briefly to let him know that a petition was being prepared asking for his release.

With the help of John Brown, editor of the *Isle of Man Times* and a JP, the petition was signed by over 3000 people and sent to the Home Secretary. Using his authority as a JP to access the prison, John Brown had managed to secure Norris's signature. Without this help Norris could not have petitioned the Home Secretary without the permission of the Governor. It is hard to believe that this permission would have been forthcoming and John Brown would feel the Governor's wrath a little later.

Farcically the reply from the Home Secretary was that the release of Samuel Norris was in the hands of the Governor's prerogative. It seemed there was no way out, so on 11 November 1916 Norris wrote directly to the Governor pointing out that he had served over three weeks, the goods the Coroner had seized had been returned, the public supported him and that his intention had only ever been to persuade the Manx Government to provide a scheme of relief preventing people from being ruined by the war. He had had no intention of committing contempt of court and he was sincerely sorry if he had done so. Finally he asked that the Governor either release him or call a court where he could appeal.

It sounds like the apology that the court had insisted upon at his trial, but it was nothing more than he had already said on that day. For whatever reason, and the hint from the Reform Campaign Committee that they would take direct action may have had something to do with it, the Governor decided to call a court to hear the application. No date for the court was set and, perhaps because it was feared there would be a demonstration, not even Norris knew of it until a couple of hours beforehand.

The proceedings of the court were ridiculous but thankfully short. Norris was granted his freedom as he was now deemed to have apologised. The *Isle of Man Times* printed an article pointing out that the apology had already been made at the trial in October and if the judges had been more reasonable 'they would have done away with the belief, which is very general both on and off the island, that the prosecution was the result of political spite, and that the court meant to commit Norris to jail, guilty or not guilty.'

Three days later John Brown received his own summons telling him to appear before the court for contempt. Perhaps learning from what he had reported about Samuel Norris, Brown chose to be very apologetic. He even said that he would never have printed the article had it come to him in time for him to give it his proper attention prior to publication. He was fined £50 and, if not paid after a period of grace, he would be imprisoned.

There was great indignation at the way Brown had been treated. Many people not only believed but had also seen first hand the lack of impartiality of the Manx judges and they did not appreciate the Governor trying to crush the freedom of the press for saying so. The fine remained unpaid and Brown was told privately that the matter had been forgotten. However, when the *Isle of Man Times* published a feature written by Samuel Norris about his imprisonment and promised further exclusive instalments, the authorities suddenly remembered and Brown felt an official hand on his shoulder.

In preparation for such an event, John Brown had kept £50 with him and was able to pay the fine immediately and avoid prison. He did not publish any more of Norris's story though, feeling it would imprudent to do so.

The second full year of the war had been a tumultuous one for the Isle of Man. In 1915 the Island had found internal divisions opening up. Financially, the towns were suffering great hardship while the country farmers were prospering. Politically, the Governor and some of his conservative friends refused to give in to the demands of an increasingly liberal thinking people. In 1916 the consequences of these divisions became obvious.

Driven by necessity, the boarding house keepers who had formed a 'league' to help each other and had tried to reason with the authorities, became a full-blown political force. No longer satisfied with fighting on just one issue, they were now demanding reform of the whole system in the Isle of Man, in keeping with the pre-war liberal changes in England. In response, the politicians took increasingly drastic action in an attempt to silence the voice of reform. If argument failed then surely prison would succeed, but all that was achieved was that each side became more convinced that they were right and the antagonism grew.

Would 1917 be a calmer year, or would the agitation continue?

CHAPTER 4

1917
Seeing it Through

By now the war was part of everyday life. The number of casualties continued rising and life at home was difficult. Food prices were high and incomes were often low. Except for inside the camps, there were few men left and the steamers that should have been bringing pleasure traffic to the island had all but disappeared and, instead, they were on war service.

In January 1917 the news reached home that the flagship of the Steam Packet fleet had been sunk. *Ben-my-Chree* was not the first Steam Packet vessel to be lost. *Empress Queen* foundered while ferrying troops across the channel and the *Ramsey* was torpedoed and sunk in 1915. However, being the flagship, the loss of *Ben-my-Chree* was a psychological blow.

The '*Ben*', as she was known, had an impressive war service record. After being fitted out as a seaplane carrier in early 1915, she was sent to the Mediterranean, where she took part in the Gallipoli campaign. While there, she made naval history when one of her seaplanes sank a Turkish supply ship, which was the first successful attack of its kind. The last British ship to leave Gallipoli, the *Ben* took part in various bombing raids in the Eastern Mediterranean and also targeted Arab camps and railways after transiting the Suez Canal.

In January 1917 she was anchored off the island of Castellorizio when a Turkish battery opened up, causing considerable damage and

Model of the Ben-my-Chree *with pictures of the interior behind, on display at the House of Manannan at Peel.*

Ben-my-Chree, *flag ship of the Steam Packet Company on fire off the Turkish coast before she sank, 1917.* Courtesy of Manx National Heritage.

setting her on fire. After five hours of shelling the burnt out wreck of *Ben-my-Chree* sank but all the crew made it safely to shore.

Less than a month later, on 5 February, another Steam Packet vessel came close to being lost. The paddle steamer *Mona's Queen* was on troop transport duty in the Channel when, just outside Le Havre, the thirty-two year old vessel became the target of a German submarine. Fortunately for the several hundred troops on board, including Lloyd George's son, the torpedo the U-boat launched missed. After this narrow escape, almost in an act of revenge, Captain Cain, who like many of the crew was Manx, issued the order for full steam ahead. It was a risk and required plenty of nerve, but it was a risk worth taking. Within minutes there was a tremendous noise as the paddles of the steamer rammed into the submarine. The U-boat sank rapidly, to the cheers of the British soldiers. It made Captain Cain and his crew heroes of the day and earned them monetary awards for their achievement.

Meanwhile, back on dry land, there was a problem involving the aliens from the camps that the Isle of Man authorities had to deal with. Trafficking between aliens and the local population was hardly new. The *Isle of Man Examiner* called the readiness with which some people had sold food and luxury items to the aliens 'a scandal' and 'unpatriotic'. Considering the difficulty the general population had in obtaining certain items, such as sugar, the paper perhaps had a point. So in February 1917 the government decided that something should be done about it.

A government circular was issued bringing to everyone's attention to the fact that prisoners of war were not allowed to leave their escorts while out in working parties. Also, it was contrary to Camp Regulations for the aliens to communicate with, make purchases from, or receive any letter, parcel or other article from the local population either directly or through their escort. Anyone caught doing so after this warning was issued was liable to prosecution under the Defence of the Realm Regulations.

The rules were pretty clear, but there were still those who either genuinely or wilfully misunderstood them, and those who were tempted to disobey either for profit or out of sympathy with the aliens' plight.

The case of Rhoda Clark, the first one since the caution was issued, was one where human sympathy was a significant factor. She had supplied some loaves of bread to aliens working near her home in

Ballaugh. As the guard was present she had thought it was fine to do so. When questioned about whether she knew that it was wrong to sell goods to aliens she said that she did know, but she had not sold the bread as she was only given the price she had paid for it – 11d.

As she spoke in her defence, Rhoda Clark mentioned that she had sons fighting and that they might be hungry. It seems as if this was the motivation behind her actions. The High Bailiff didn't take too much pity on her, although he described her actions as 'thoughtless' rather than deliberate. He could not understand how anyone could deal with the aliens, it was as if their very existence was repugnant to him. He decided that a fine of £1 would suffice in this case.

Other cases were not dealt with so leniently. Arthur Breadner worked in the camp canteens. At 51 years he had been on war service until he was discharged as no longer fit, and prior to the war he had run a boarding house in Douglas. Despite having excellent character witnesses and pleading guilty, the High Bailiff was not inclined to show much mercy. Arthur had never been in trouble before and had been under some pressure to procure whiskey for the alien Dieckmann. This was the only time he had given in and, misunderstanding the gravity of the offence, he had expected, if caught, to be dismissed but nothing worse. No doubt abusing his position as a camp employee did not impress and the High Bailiff sent him to jail for three months.

The case of farmer James Allen was dealt with differently. He had been selling goods to the aliens in an established practice of taking orders from notes left in known hiding places and depositing the goods where the camp internees would find them. He openly admitted his guilt and tried to buy his way out of trouble by offering security of £600 for his future good conduct. As a farmer, the 36-year-old Allen was at the time exempt from service, but when his case came before the High Bailiff it was adjourned for a fortnight. This was to give Allen the chance to enlist. If he did not, the High Bailiff would impose a substantial term of imprisonment.

It was not just trafficking that was seen as bad, but aiding the aliens in any way could result in prosecution as one lady, Sarah Anne Radcliffe, found to her cost. In August 1917 Mrs Radcliffe was brought before the High Bailiff on two counts. First she was charged with failing to answer police questions to the best of her knowledge and, secondly, she had knowingly harboured or assisted two escaped prisoners of war, Otto Rohreig and Jan Voight. The two prisoners had escaped from the Douglas camp and the police were alerted. As was usual, it did not take long to find them. On the morning of the recapture, Sarah Radcliffe visited a local inn and, while there, she was approached by one of the aliens, who asked if she would be willing to provide him with lunch if he paid for it. He claimed to be Welsh and, as he had been wounded, he was taking something of a holiday on the island just as he had before the war. As he was walking around the island and staying in different places he could not eat at his lodgings and, as he explained, he was wearing civilian clothes as he had a permit to do so. Naively, Sarah fell for the story and agreed to make the lunch, not realising that it was actually lunch for two until she returned to the inn to let the man know it was ready. Unfortunately, one of the men decided to go in search of tobacco and it was at this point that he was arrested.

Sarah served lunch to the remaining man but while he was there she received a message to say that he might be a camp escapee. She challenged the man and tried to make him leave the house but failed to do so before the police arrived. Maybe because she was flustered, or frightened by having an internee in the house and the consequences of that, she appeared to the police, to be obstructive. She had been asked if there was a strange man in the house and she had replied 'no'. In court she said that she had been asked if there was any man 'upstairs', which, in her excited state, might have been what she heard. Ultimately though, answering 'no' to the question condemned her on the charge of not answering the police questions.

On the second charge, knowingly harbouring aliens, she fared no better. Several people had witnessed the men speak and claimed that it was not possible to tell that they were foreign as their English was so good. Also, there was some doubt as to whether it would have been common knowledge that morning that two aliens had escaped. The prosecutors and the High Bailiff did not agree. Sarah was found guilty and fined £1 for not answering police questions, and sent to jail for a month for harbouring aliens. Upon sentence being pronounced Sarah collapsed but was removed to the prison as soon as she recovered. Some believed Sarah and all traffickers were unpatriotic, but maybe some were simply caught out by the law and the changed circumstances of an extreme event such as war.

Changes in the law also caught holidaymaker Charles Sayers of Liverpool, who foolishly claimed to be German prior to boarding the steamer home. Since war had broken out it had been the duty of the ticket inspector, under the Admiralty restrictions, to ask the nationality of anyone who wished to board the steamers. Probably finding the idea that he could be anything other than British ridiculous, Sayers had jokingly answered that he was German. While his wife was allowed to sail home, he was brought before the JP and fined 10s with 5s costs and imprisoned for seven days. He said he was very sorry for what he had done, having no idea he would be taken seriously, but it was the lecture from his wife once he returned home that he was more fearful of than either the fine or the prison sentence.

Another victim of the Defence of the Realm Regulations was Wilmer Bounds. He was an associate of Samuel Norris and had acted as chairman of the reform committee. In March 1917 he was brought before the High Bailiff on a charge of making false statements.

At a meeting of the Reform Campaign held in March 1917, he had brought a resolution calling the Home Secretary's attention to the failure of the Governor to apply the Potatoes (Maximum Prices) Order to the island, and to the commandeering of potatoes by the Manx Government for use at the aliens' camps. The latter statement had been based on a newspaper report and a telegram sent to the wholesale farmers' market from the Government Office. The government had asked for two hundred tons of potatoes and were willing to pay £9 per ton plus half a ton of basic slag. This meant the government was offering about £11 per ton, which was £2 per ton more than the maximum price in England. To Bounds and others, it looked as if the government was buying up potatoes at a high price for the camps and thereby forcing the price up for locals and limiting availability.

However, Mr Bounds, influenced by a report in the *Isle of Man Times*, had been mistaken in his conclusions. The government had wanted to buy the potatoes to ensure that they were available for the local population at a time when they anticipated there would be a shortage. Mr Bounds was also wrong in his belief that potatoes for the camps were either bought by the Manx Government or sourced from the island. Add to this his known hostility towards the government and, although he denied it, the Governor personally, it was unlikely that the High Bailiff would find in his favour.

The evidence given in court showed that Bounds had not taken the time to find out the truth of the matter before he had brought the resolution forward. In particular, in the resolution Bounds had used the word 'commandeering', when the government had only actually 'asked' for the potatoes. At a stretch of the imagination, he claimed that as 'commandeer' was not a word in the dictionary he could only say that it would mean to take control of, not take by force. It is hard to believe that Bounds did not know the meaning of the word 'commandeer', and it is hard to argue that he did not make a false statement. Equally it is hard to say that it was worthwhile prosecuting someone for telling a 'lie' when it really did not affect anyone. The report in the paper had already made similar statements public and it had not caused any specific mass disaffection, which was the main concern behind the regulation.

Following in the footsteps of Ambrose Qualtrough, who had gone to prison for a breach of DORA, Bounds was found guilty. He was fined £2 or seven days' imprisonment. Perhaps learning from past mistakes the authorities did not make a martyr out of him and the fine was paid by the Reform Campaign, probably because they realised that in effect he was guilty.

Within days of the troublesome resolution being passed, the Governor prohibited the export of potatoes from the island and a government scheme to supply potatoes to the civil population was established, along with reduced rations given to the alien camps. Reading Samuel Norris's memoirs, he makes it sound as though this was a small victory for the reformers. However, coming so soon after the public meeting, and judging by the past resistance of the authorities to the activities of the reform movement, it is unlikely that the resolution had any effect and in all probability the decision had already been made.

Food, in general, was becoming another battle ground. In England various essentials, such as butter, sugar and meats, would be formally rationed in 1918 and prices fixed by the government. On the Isle of Man, despite control of foods, sugar alone was rationed. However, the price of foodstuffs had risen by sixty per cent. This meant that for those who were rich enough there was plenty to be had but, for many, food, a basic necessity, was becoming a luxury.

The anonymous 'Really Disgusted' wrote to the *Isle of Man*

Examiner about the problem. 'We read about food economy and meatless days, but I think it is high time that rationing among them that can live without working should become compulsory, for I know for a fact that on one place there is more meat given to the pet dogs in a week than any six farm workers in the district get for a month.' 'Really Disgusted' concluded that if he, or she, had the money they would not be so unpatriotic as to keep maids and pets to be consuming the food that working men should have.

'Justice', another anonymous letter writer, this time to the *Ramsey Courier* wrote on a similar theme concerning the low wages of farm labourers. He did not want lectures on how to economize but wanted to know how to support a family on the wages paid when the price of essentials was so high. He finished the letter with the following observation: 'We are sacrificing all these lives and money fighting Germany for Right and Justice. Let us practise it in our own island.' The *Ramsey Courier* printed this letter and claimed to have received several others on the subject, which it had entitled 'Manx White Slavery'.

Many people were now not just financially pressed but were facing the real danger of hunger. At this time this would cause annoyance and concern, but later it would erupt into direct action. Perhaps it would have served the authorities well to have taken the message in such letters to the papers on board.

One consequence of the relative availability of food was that visitors to the island were amazed by the goods on sale in the shops. In 1917 visitor numbers had increased, although nothing like the hundreds of thousands that had been seen before the war. Some visitors and some residents too, smuggled items such as small joints of beef, sugar or butter to friends in England. The Manx authorities tended to turn a blind eye to this as long as it was only on a small scale. According to Samuel Norris's memoirs, only one visitor was arrested and brought before a magistrate for smuggling. Walking down the pier with a whole leg of mutton openly displayed under his arm was just too obvious.

For the locals it was bread that was to bring about the most agitation. The re-emergence of unrestricted submarine warfare by Germany in early 1917 brought disruption to the food chain and, at one point, left England with only six weeks of wheat supplies. War conditions had meant that the price of bread had risen drastically. To combat this, the British Government introduced the subsidized loaf. The Governor had asked if the Isle of Man was to be included in the scheme. The late and brief reply he received was that it was up to him to look after the Manx 9d loaf (9d being the price fixed), as he was Chancellor of the Manx Exchequer.

Of course many islanders wanted the 9d loaf, but the Governor was less enthusiastic. At a meeting of Tynwald he said that to introduce the subsidy would cost about £42,000 a year. He proposed two other schemes for consideration. The first, to ration bread and pay the subsidy on that amount only, leaving any excess required to be paid for at the full price, was estimated would cost about £20,000 a year. The second was to issue bread tickets to those who could prove they were in need, which would entitle them to a loaf of bread at 9d. It was thought this would cost about £12,000.

The Governor also asked Tynwald to consider that new taxation may well have to be raised to cover the cost; in effect, income tax. However, with little regard for the maths involved, he also said that income tax would raise very little money while the amount needed to subsidize bread would be enormous. As usual, the Governor seemed to be oblivious to the revenues being generated, which for the year 1916-17 had been over £120,000, with nearly half of that coming from excisable items consumed at the camps. He also greatly overestimated government expenditure, which for the same year had been over £90,000 less than expected.

Ultimately the question of the bread subsidy was left to a committee. The committee took about a month to gather evidence from various groups, such as trade organisations, working class representatives, and even the Reform Campaign Committee. The evidence for adopting the subsidy scheme as it was in England was overwhelming.

The pauperising scheme of issuing bread tickets was ridiculed. At a public meeting of the Workers' Union held that September, a resolution was passed protesting at the scheme, demanding the English subsidy and that the revenue to fund it should be met with income tax. They also resolved that the Governor be requested to take steps to control food prices on the Isle of Man. No doubt the unsettled weather that had caused problems for the harvest only added to their concerns.

The Workers' Union was only formed in March 1917. Although its formation had happened quietly, about 1000 people attended the September meeting and the Union would become a significant political force.

As for the Reform Campaign Committee, Samuel Norris, as their secretary, had spoken for them on the question of bread. He was asked which he would prefer; old age pensions or bread at 9d, as it would not be possible to support both. To this he replied that if social services on the Isle of Man could not be brought in line with those in England, his Committee would press for annexation.

After all the evidence had been gathered, in early October the Legislature brought in the 9d loaf bread subsidy. To finance this, the Governor put forward £20,000 from the accumulated fund. The Home Secretary gave his approval, limited to six months, on the condition that the cost was met by new taxation. The Governor accepted this and, surprisingly, given his conservative nature, he put forward a Bill to impose income tax. It would still be some time before this tax passed into law.

It looked as if the Reform Campaign now had allies in the form of the Workers' Union and that they were both making a little progress towards their goals. For the Reform Campaign, 1917 had been another busy, but frustrating year.

Early in the year they had tried to bring about reform of the Manx legal system. This had been an aim of the original reform movement set up in 1903 and did have some logic behind it. With the Governor and the Deemsters unlikely to find fault with each other, appeals, for example, were unlikely to have fair hearings. When Thomas Kneen, Clerk of the Rolls, the first judge of the Manx High Court, died in November 1916 it left a vacancy and an opportunity. The Reform Campaign Committee lost little time in preparing a resolution for the Home Secretary. They asked him to abolish the vacant position and carry out the reform recommendations of the MacDonnell Commission, which had been pushed aside on account of the war, and appoint an English barrister as Manx Judge of Appeal. It would be the only effective way to remove bias.

On 27 February 1917, a Bill to reform the judicial system was brought before the Legislative Council. It was explained that the Bill had been drawn up by the Home Office and sent to them to carry into law. The Governor claimed he had done his utmost to get the Home

Office to wait until after the war but his arguments had fallen on deaf ears. The Bill was treated with contempt by the legal members of the Council and it was postponed so that they could ascertain the views of the Manx Law Society.

The postponement ended up being nearly nine months, during which time the Bill was ignored. It fell once again to Samuel Norris and his committee to remind, or inform, the Home Secretary that the Bill had not yet been dealt with. Within a week, under the instructions of the Home Office, the Legislative Council, who had met hurriedly behind closed doors, brought the Bill forward again. A month later it received Royal assent and became law. It had taken a long time, but slowly there was the promise that things could be changed to improve the lives of the general population. Two years later the Governor was also removed from the bench.

The Reform Campaign were obviously delighted with this turn of events. However, it had taken a long time and they had been far from idle since Samuel Norris had been released from prison. For a second year running they held a demonstration at the Tynwald Day ceremony. This demonstration was not as large scale as that of the previous year and it did not have the same impact. They passed many of the same, or similar, resolutions, calling for income tax and old age pensions, but they did not generate the same interest. Speeches were made denouncing the legislature, but how much notice was taken this time divided the opinion of the newspapers.

A second event happened that summer, and for a moment islanders were able to escape from the hardships of war. Hall Caine's famous novel of the day, *The Manxman*, had been made into a film and was shown at the Villa Marina in August. Hall Caine is practically unheard of today, but at the time he was one of the most popular authors. He was born in Cheshire but his father was Manx. He returned to the island and in 1896 bought Greeba Castle.

The Manxman was one of his greatest successes. It was published in 1894, sold half a million copies and was translated into several languages. As its title suggests, it was set on the Isle of Man, and the previous year the London Film Company filmed it on the Island. A review in the *Isle of Man Examiner* did warn, though, that many of the people who had flocked around the cameras in the hope of seeing themselves on film would be disappointed. Many such scenes had either been cut or did not leave time to identify anyone. If human behaviour around a film crew has not changed much in a century, neither has local support for local work. The two hours and twenty minutes of film were shown to a 'spellbound' audience, which included the Governor and his wife.

Such respites from the war did not last long though. The authorities had begun the year trying to control the internee population and, as the autumn drew in, they needed to do so again.

The censors at the Knockaloe Camp found marked naval maps of the Irish Sea in the false bottom of a box sent to one of the prisoners. At about the same time, so the story goes, two men working in a large factory in the north of England were overheard having a conversation. It is claimed that they said that six enemy submarines would be in the north Irish Sea between 29 March and 2 April 1918. They would attack

Inside a hut at Knockaloe. Courtesy of Manx National Heritage.

every vessel except one from the Isle of Man, which would have a large number of German prisoners from the Knockaloe Camp on board.

As a result of the maps being found, precautions were taken and effectively any chance of escape was ruled out. Whether or not the story of the overheard conversation is true, Bertrand Sargeaunt, the Government Secretary, made a note of it in his memoirs of the war, giving it some credibility. The only thing that can be said with any certainty is that between the dates mentioned there was a certain amount of U-boat activity in the vicinity of the island and one of them torpedoed the White Star liner *Celtic*.

Many of the conditions of war were now commonplace. Everything from the camps, to the grief of a lost loved one, to the unaffordable price of food were just part of everyday life. The latter, of course, was a guaranteed way to bring about public discontent. By the end of 1917, the authorities were probably quite used to political agitation and, at times, such as when they were forced to accept an English appeal judge, they had had to capitulate. However, they were surprisingly blind to the strength of the political forces against them, and to their cost they never even attempted, even partially, to meet the demands of the people.

CHAPTER 5

1918
The Final Blows

Unsuspected by most, the final year of the war would bring about much change for the people of the Island and, direct action, far from dying down, would be most effective.

In February a meeting was held. This meeting gathered together delegates of the various trade unions and societies of the island, and they were there to progress the formation of a Manx Labour Party.

Their objectives, as recorded in the *Isle of Man Times*, were:

'(a) To unite the forces of Labour within the Isle of Man, and to secure the return of Labour representatives on all legislative and administrative bodies.

'(b) To secure for the producers by hand or by brain the full fruits of their industry, and the most equitable distribution thereof that may be possible, upon the basis of the common ownership of the means of production and the best obtainable system of popular administration and control of each industry or service.

'(c) Generally to promote the political, social and economic emancipation of the people.

'(d) To give effect as far as possible to the principles from time to time approved by the Party Conference.'

It was the first time that an organised political party was in existence on the Island.

Mr H.M. Emery was appointed secretary. He made a speech at the meeting saying how the war had given them the impetus to take the ideas that 'had spent generations in the heads of men' and make those ideas a reality in the fields of politics and industry. He pointed out how peace would bring as many problems as war, and he called reconstruction 'a burning question' to which everyone would demand democratic answers.

Shortly after this meeting, 'Walter C' wrote an impassioned and near fanatical article for the *Isle of Man Examiner*, extolling the utopian virtues of the socialist regime that the machinery of the Labour Party would put in place. There would not be just be a few reforms or a few seats gained in the House of Keys, but true equality of responsibility, a lack of selfishness and law and order to prevent, not cause, oppression. Everyone, except the unworthy propertied classes, would be included, as they would realise the power they possess, and men would be like women – unashamed of sentiment. The reality, however, would be quite different.

That September, though, did see the first Manx Labour Party conference, where they affiliated themselves with the English Labour Party and put forward resolutions that would effectively become their manifesto. The resolutions called for various things, including the redistribution of seats in the Keys, the nationalization of steamship and railway companies, old age pensions, a forty-eight hour week and national health insurance.

The lack of social care, such as old age pensions, was the main reason that annexation had been called for in the past, and the Labour Party wanted to put the Manx people on an equal footing with the English. Of particular annoyance was the fact that soldiers who had gone to fight had paid national insurance on their pay but if they returned to the Isle of Man they would forfeit any benefit in terms of pension or compensation.

The resolutions passed at the conference were far more rooted in reality than the ethereal message of 'Walter C', but the rhetoric and language used was just as zealous. Curiously, they did make one rather unfortunate mistake in relation to the call for a forty-eight hour week.

A Mr Dickinson claimed that in Ramsey there was a philanthropic association that made girls, after a day's work, carry home big piles of stockings and socks to finish, which robbed them of any life as it often kept them working until after midnight. The association he was referring to was the Manx Industries Association which, considering it had achieved more in real terms in alleviating war distress than either the authorities or the Labour Party, was completely the wrong target.

Needless to say, Copeland-Smith totally refuted these allegations. In a letter to *Mona's Herald* he made it clear that working hours were forty-nine and a half per week and that the girls only took work home with them to finish at their own request. He also included a letter from the workers to the directors which read:

'We, the undersigned workers of the Ramsey branch of the Manx Industries Association take this opportunity to thank the directors for so kindly conceding our request by extending the working hours from 6 o'clock to 6.30 each evening. We wish the directors to know that Mr Dickinson did not in any way express our sentiments at the Labour Conference held in Douglas. We greatly appreciated the privilege which had until recently been granted to us, ie, of taking our work home.'

Another criticism from the Labour Party Conference was that shirt makers in England had been given a 5½d per hour pay rise. Alfred Teare, who made this comment, claimed that he had been incorrectly reported and that he had said that shirt makers in England had had their wages increased to 5½d per hour. This was frequently what the girls were earning through their piecework rate and whether Copeland-Smith believed Alfred Tear's claim is left unclear in his letter.

Certainly the Manx Industries Association had done very well. In August they held their third annual meeting. It was reported that during that year the number of employees had increased by twenty-five per cent, but that the wages had doubled to a cost of some £20,000 per annum. They had manufactured over a million pairs of socks and had opened two new branches. The venture had been a big success story during the war and it was intended that the work would continue in peace time. The directors were duly appointed for life and the basis of the company, that no dividends or bonus could be paid to shareholders and instead all profits had to be used for the good of the employees or the people of the island, was reaffirmed.

Regardless of the rights and wrongs of the Labour Party, there was a hardening of the attitude of the working classes which, in 1918, boiled over into several episodes of industrial action.

On 20 April, miners at the Laxey mine ceased work. For some years the mine had been in trouble but was just about the only form of employment in the locality. The miners had requested a rise in pay the previous November but this had not been granted. The finances of the mine showed that from 1 April 1917 to 31 March 1918 over £11,000 had been paid in wages but profits had been less than £250. Not unreasonably, the directors came to the conclusion that it would be impossible to increase wages.

As a result of this notification, the workers of the mine staged a strike, claiming that they had exhausted every method of mediation. The miners had asked for an advance of nearly 15s a week, which from the accounts was clearly impossible. The financial position of the mine was precarious and a strike would not help. Once the famous Laxey Wheel was stopped for any length of time, water accumulated at the lower levels. At the time it was unlikely that the company would have been able to raise the necessary funds to cover the cost of draining the mine.

The Isle of Man branch of the Workers' Union was affiliated to the Manchester district. The Manchester chairman, Councillor George Titt was fully involved with, and supported, the strike action at the mine. Councillor Titt had visited the island and met the workers. He had encouraged them and blamed the directors for the situation.

Both Titt and the chairman of directors of the mine met with the Minister of Munitions, who was to arbitrate. The minister's orders were that all the men working at the wheel and the pumps were to resume work immediately and the rest as soon as possible. The decision on pay was to be postponed until the men returned to work and it was later reported that the 15s pay rise was accepted. The cost of the pay rise was to fall on the British Government, not the mine.

At the same time as the Laxey miners were striking, the Douglas gas workers were also threatening strike action. They had been offered a 2s a week war bonus which they had refused saying they wanted 5s. The workers and the company agreed to the arbitration of the

Government Secretary and, with the gas workers being awarded nearly everything they asked for, the matter was settled.

By far the most widespread action taken that year, though, was in July, and it was known as the Bread Strike.

Taxation and the provision of social services had been a continuing argument from before the war. In April the government increased indirect taxation on tobacco, spirits and beer. Of income tax, despite a bill having been sent to the Keys the previous October, nothing was heard.

In fact a committee had been appointed and had taken information and advice from various groups. These included the English Inland Revenue, the politicians who claimed that income tax was pointless on the island as so few businesses were open, and farmers who claimed they could not be expected to keep books. By April the committee was ready to put forward its recommendations and amendments to the Bill. Crucially, one of the amendments was a clause stating that all revenue from income tax must come under the control of Tynwald, and the British Government would not have any say in how the money was to be used.

This style of clause had already been used to great effect the previous year when it prevented the Estate Duties Bill from receiving Royal assent. On that occasion they had stipulated that the revenue had to be used for old age pensions. Now they were not specifying any particular use for the revenue, but the Keys did want to have the final say in how it was spent. The British Government, which already had a say in how the island used the duties raised, would never have accepted that level of independence.

Knowing the effect that this had had on the proposed estate duties, there can be little doubt that while some MHKs wanted to see greater economic freedom for the island, some would have seen this as an opportunity to prevent income tax becoming law.

Unfortunately time was running out. The bread subsidy, which had kept a loaf of bread at 9d, was only authorised for six months until a new tax could be raised. In fact the subsidy lasted about eight months as the money put aside from the accumulated fund was enough to fund the extra time.

On Friday, 28 June the Governor presented the budget to Tynwald. It showed a surplus of £40,000, making the accumulated fund £94,000 and it had all come from indirect taxes. A substantial amount of this would have come from supplying the camps and would have been paid by the British Government. It was clear that once the war came to an end and the camps removed, if the holiday trade did not pick up the island could be very vulnerable financially. As it happened, visitor numbers in 1918 were the highest they had been since before the war and some of those visitors would play a part in what happened next.

As the Governor continued his budget speech, he said that as far as taxation was concerned they had reached a 'blind alley'. He agreed in principle that the island should determine how its own taxes were spent, but if that all important clause prevented the Bill from receiving Royal assent the bread subsidy would cease. The Governor had already been to London to try and ease the passage of the Bill but he had failed, so it was left in the hands of the Keys.

The Keys retired to their own chamber to discuss the matter and resolved that the bread subsidy should continue until March 1919 and should be financed by the accumulated fund. They also refused to grant any indirect taxation until the subsidy question was settled.

This left the Governor with little choice. The subsidy had to come to an end and so it was announced by the bakers that as of Monday, 1 July a loaf would be priced at 1s. Under DORA, the Governor tried to fix the price at 10½d, but the bakers said that they could not produce a loaf under a shilling unless they were subsidised and refused to bake until the matter was settled.

The news that the 9d load was to stop was greeted with dismay. The Legislative Council made appeals to the Keys to pass the Bill without the clause and postpone the fight for greater control to another time. Well-attended open air meetings were held throughout the island and it was the MHKs who were blamed for their failure to pass the bill.

The meeting that Sunday on the Douglas foreshore was described in *Mona's Herald* as an assembly of about 1500 people where there was 'a complete absence of opposition'. There were several speakers that afternoon, including Alfred Tear, Secretary of the Douglas branch of the Workers' Union, Mr Emery, Secretary of the Manx Labour Party and Samuel Norris. They were universal in their condemnation of the Keys. They had no interest in the various quarrels between the politicians and the bakers regarding the subsidy, or between the politicians and the British Government regarding control of revenue.

They wanted the 9d loaf and income tax to pay for it. If their demands were not met they would stage a strike. For once they did not blame the Governor, who they said had been honest in his dealings with them.

It was expected that when Tynwald met the following Tuesday the 9d loaf would be reinstated. However, the Keys were not prepared to compromise and simply reaffirmed their position. They were not prepared to give up their birth right as they saw it. Mr Cormode, MHK, even went as far as to say that if the people of the island were willing to sign their rights away then the MHKs should be sent back to their constituencies, where the people could either return them or return someone who was willing to do the Governor's bidding.

From this point the strike was inevitable in the eyes of the workers' leaders. On the Wednesday evening, Alfred Tear, now chairman of the newly formed Strike Committee, presided over a public meeting attended by several thousand people. The Strike Committee had already consulted with the Governor and other officials, and Alfred Tear spoke of their efforts to avoid a strike. He spoke of their determination to gain equal rights with workers in England and proposed that as the Keys had held up the Income Tax Bill, the strikers should contact the Labour members of the British Government and ask it to impose the tax.

The impending strike was called a moral strike and the leaders asked for those taking part to act in an orderly fashion. It was promised that all essential public services would not be interfered with and after several rousing speeches the meeting dispersed. There were a few people who tried to persuade the strikers of the errors of their ways but these were greatly outnumbered. It was the eve of a battle and an air of excitement pervaded the town.

The next day most of the island came to a standstill. Although a few bread shops in the poorer areas of town were allowed to open between 7.00 am and 9.00 am and a Peel fishing boat was allowed to land its herring and sell them very cheaply to the poor, the vast majority of shops and workshops were closed. Any establishment that did open was visited by the strikers and had its workers ejected. The gas works were closed and all trams, trains and motor vehicles were stopped, as was the daily steamer to Liverpool.

The steamer from Liverpool had been allowed to sail on the understanding that the return journey would not be allowed until the strike was over. There were about 500 visitors on the sailing who might not be able to go home. There were also visitors on the island who were hoping to go home for the weekend and were effectively stranded. As a result they played their own part in the strike.

By nine o'clock it was clear that the holidaymakers were going to interfere. They held a protest meeting at the Jubilee Clock, near the pier and decided that a deputation should meet with both the strike leaders and the Governor. Six gentlemen were appointed and one speaker suggested that if no satisfactory settlement was agreed upon they should go through Strand Street smashing windows. What he hoped to gain from this is unclear. Some speakers said that the island owed a debt to the English visitor who so kindly came over and spent his money, and another reportedly said that the Manx were 'simply a lot of b****** swine!'

Such comments, which the journalist from *Mona's Herald* said were made 'with that delightful tact which makes a certain class of Englishman so popular wherever he goes', gave rise to some heated debates between strikers and visitors. The strikers felt they were justified in preventing the steamer from leaving, while the visitors, some of whom, needed to return for war work, saw no reason why they should be the ones to suffer.

The Governor had promised them a boat if at all possible and the visitors took it upon themselves to telegraph their own MPs describing their predicament. Despite differing points of view there was little trouble. One gentleman, however, did find himself in a fight, but luckily he was rescued by his friends who persuaded him not provoke the strikers.

The only other incident of any severity happened down on the Douglas quayside. Captain Moughtin MHK, who had shown himself to be less than sympathetic to those suffering war distress, refused to close his coal dealing business. As a result of this, stones were thrown through his windows breaking glass and damaging the furniture within. The police attended but they were overwhelmed by the crowd and thankfully, a strike leader appeared in time to mediate. For his own safety, Captain Moughtin was taken to the local police station.

As there was no transport, the Tynwald ceremony that should have been held the next day was cancelled. As the crowds grew and there were rumours of gangs likely to loot, the Governor closed all public houses.

The 'success' of the strike not only shocked everyone, but also brought its own problems. The Thursday would normally have been a half-day for shop keepers and the Friday should have been a public holiday with pay. No one had really thought about what would happen if the strike continued into the Saturday or beyond. Employers had expected their employees back for the Saturday. If businesses failed to open then not only might they fail to stay in business but the people could not be fed. The Governor had tried, but failed, to get the strike leaders to modify their demands. They would have the 9d loaf, an undertaking that no striker would be victimised for their part during the day and no other compromise. The end of the strike though, when it did come, was still unexpected.

A meeting of the strikers was called for three o'clock on the Friday afternoon. It had been rumoured that there was an important announcement to be made. At the appointed time a great crowd gathered at the Jubilee Clock and after a signal, silence fell to hear what the strike leaders had to say. 'We got it!' Alf Tear cried to the jubilation of those gathered. In truth, capitulation was the only viable option open to Lord Raglan, and the fact that he agreed with the strikers that the House of Keys was the problem probably aided his decision.

After lengthy interviews with the Governor it had been agreed that the 9d loaf would be reinstated, there would be no victimisation against strikers and the strike would be lifted. The leaders still warned that although everyone could now go back to work, if there were any problems in carrying out the agreement between the Governor and the Committee, the strike would begin again. The Governor was applauded for doing his utmost to find a solution to the situation and the Keys carried all the blame. The picture houses and the pubs opened again and an evening of celebration began.

The strike was meant to be across the whole island but it had its main success in Douglas. In some areas it did not really begin until the Friday, and several hundred people still travelled to St John's not knowing that the Tynwald ceremony had been postponed.

The strike may have been over but the question of income tax had still not been settled. The next day the Governor left the island for London. Relations between the Home Office and Lord Raglan had not always been as cordial as they could have been and it is likely that the meetings that took place that July were difficult. Whatever was actually said during those days, the Home Secretary certainly took notice of the various resolutions that had been sent to him by the different social and political groups on the island. The Governor returned with detailed instructions for income tax. He was given a week to have the Income Tax Bill signed or it would be imposed by the British Government.

Among the conditions set, the tax had to be imposed retrospectively to the previous April and the first £130 was to be exempt. Possibly in reaction to the Governor insisting that an income tax would bring very little in and so would hardly be worth it, the Home Secretary also set the scale. In all other respects the Bill remained the same as the one the Governor had sent to the Keys the previous autumn.

The legislature of the island now had no choice. The bill had to be passed. When the Home Secretary had set the stepped scale he had specified the first few bands and then used the phrase 'and so on'. This phrase was then used to bring about some self-determination. It was not a specific instruction and, improbably, the Governor, unchallenged by any member of the legislature, claimed not to know what it meant. As a result, the scale was stopped at incomes of £1500 a year.

The House of Keys were at first chastened and accepted the Bill. However, completely ignoring their own responsibility, they soon changed their minds and criticized the Governor for mishandling the situation and forcing them to impose taxes at twice the necessary rate to provide for the 9d loaf.

Even to the last hour the debate raged. Finally, the Governor agreed to an altered scale on the condition that a special clause was added. This clause would give him the ability to impose enough tax the following year to cover both that year's bread subsidy and any deficit for the current year. This was one way the Keys could bring about a little self-determination but it did give the much criticized Governor extraordinary power.

The Bill was eventually signed on 18 July 1918. It was the first income tax and the first direct tax to be imposed on the island. For some it was a glorious victory and the special powers that had been given to the Governor were never needed. The tax raised more than enough income to cover the bread subsidy and the rates were lowered the following year. It would be many years before the rates of income tax would be as high as those set by the Home Secretary.

The belated Tynwald ceremony took place on 1 August, unmarred by the demonstrations of the previous years. It was also held at a time when the island was just beginning to see an influx of visitors again. For the weekend of 27 July, Douglas was once again crowded. The promenade looked like it was part of the season and the shops were busy. Similar reports came from other parts of the island and by the Saturday there was a shortage of food and prices soared. As the *Ramsey Courier* remarked, it was a profiteer's paradise. The Governor had refused to fix prices and visitors indulged in the freedom of unrestricted sales, so alien to their rationed homeland.

Post-war reconstruction had been spoken about publically for several months, but the visitor numbers that weekend was perhaps the first tangible sign that the island could recover. Over the course of the 1918 season about 97,000 visitors came. Although nowhere close to the figures of the pre-war years it was a good sign that the re-emergence of the season, so critical to recovery, would happen.

However, there was still the prospect of another winter to survive. It was expected that there would be a shortage of fuel and, in order to save coal, The Early Closing Order was issued. It was believed that closing shops early would save fuel for lighting and heating, and it was a system that was in operation in England. The practice of moving the clocks by an hour in the spring and autumn to save daylight had been in operation since 1916.

An earlier finishing time might sound attractive, but for some it was cause for concern. To close a shop at 6.00 pm or 7.00 pm, instead of 8.00 pm, could mean a loss of business, or that the working classes would be unable to purchase provisions after their working day had finished.

The case of the barbers was highlighted as a particular problem. Barbers' patrons would be employed throughout the day, not leaving work until 6.00 pm - the very hour that the hairdressing and shaving salons must close. Therefore, the only opportunity for men to visit the barbers would be a Saturday afternoon, causing great congestion. It might sound whimsical, but a frequent visit to the barbers was a genuine part of life. It was serious enough for the Governor to allow barbers to stay open until 7.00 pm four nights a week.

The Government Office informed the *Isle of Man Examiner* that the first week of early closing saved about twenty-one tons of coal, and as the days shortened it would be expected that that saving would increase. However the *Isle of Man Times* took a slightly different view. On the first day of the order being in operation, the paper claimed shops were compelled to close in perfect weather and broad daylight, and that they would be saving gas that would never have been used. The paper concluded, 'DORA is responsible for a lot of unnecessary nonsense in these days'.

Eight weeks later the Armistice was signed. The news of the end of the war was received in Douglas by telegraph from the Eiffel Tower at precisely 11.00 am on 11 November. A great relief and, in theory, a cause for celebration, services of thanksgiving were held throughout the island.

By the end of the war 8,261 Manxmen had answered the call to arms. This was eighty-two per cent of the serviceable population and one of the highest percentages within the Empire. Of these, 1165 were killed on the battlefields and over 1000 were injured or taken prisoner. There were over 260 decorations, including two Victoria Crosses. It was a large sacrifice for a small island which suffered not only the loss of its men, but also its lifeline as only three of the requisitioned Steam Packet Company vessels were able to return to normal service.

It was quite an honour when, on 21 November, the German High Seas Fleet sailed into captivity with the Steam Packet's *King Orry* leading the German warships to the surrender.

Any pleasure taken in victory was unfortunately blemished by the earlier outbreak of the influenza epidemic. Whereas fatal cases were few compared to England, there were at least eighty-eight people who lost their lives over the course of the winter. Among the flu victims was Alexander Gill, the far-sighted developer who built many of the boarding houses and whose assistance to tenants, particularly in reducing rents during the war, was much appreciated.

Despite the perils of flu, 3000 people still attended a celebration and thanksgiving gathering at the Villa Marina. There were two speakers that day, Sir Hall Caine and the Governor. Considering Hall Caine had had relatively little to do with the island's affairs for some time he was perhaps a strange choice of speaker at such a public meeting. However, drawing on his skills as a writer, he managed to put the grief that many were suffering into words and painted a portrait of how it would be to live as one of the many injured. Following on from a point the Governor had already made, he believed that everything possible would be done for those who were returning from the theatres of war.

The Governor may have had a lack of ability to grasp the financial aspects of the island at times, but at the hour of victory he was unfailing in his knowledge as a soldier. In his speech that day he managed to find just the right tone for the occasion. He mixed his military knowledge with pride in victory and remembrance of those who would not be coming back. He also reminded everyone that it would be an arduous road back to where they were before the war, and he appealed for support to the various charities that could offer help to the families of the fallen or those who were injured. In many respects it was one of the Governor's finer moments.

It was clear that reconstruction was at the forefront of the Governor's mind, just as it was for many others. At the same time he was being installed as a Grand Master of a new Freemason's Lodge and was promising to do everything he could to support the Lodge over the next twelve months. The island had no inkling of the events that were to unfold and perhaps, on 16 November at the Freemason's Lodge, even the Governor himself was unaware of what would happen next.

The Governor knew that reconstruction would be an enormous and difficult task. He also knew that the already strained relations with the British Government were unlikely to improve. They had confirmed that Manx Reform Bills would proceed 'after the war', but the Governor was directly opposed to such measures.

Part of the British Government's demobilization plans was to provide soldiers, sailors and munitions workers returning to civilian life with a grant during unemployment. The Governor was expected to bring a similar scheme into being in the Isle of Man and brought the matter before Tynwald. Without health and unemployment insurance already available on the island, the cost of such a scheme would be greater. The Governor hugely overestimated the cost and thought that it could be as high as £60,000 or even £70,000. Perhaps this was just scaremongering, but he did ask for a first vote of £20,000.

As the war had been fought on behalf of the British and the island had sacrificed much, Lord Raglan was also of the belief that such provision should be met by the British, not the Manx Government. He was not alone in this belief either. Several members of the Keys were of the same opinion and the Governor, encouraging them, offered to put forward any resolution of protest they might pass, even though the British Government had made its position quite clear.

Financially, the island was very healthy by the end of the war. Customs duties and taxes had far outpaced expenditure, and the British Government alone had paid millions for the construction of the camps, their upkeep, the people employed there and in customs duties on various items consumed by the internees. After fighting and paying for a war that also benefitted the Manx people, it is understandable that the British Government would want the island to take some responsibility for returning soldiers who might not find employment so quickly.

It is possible that this brewing argument, which the island was unlikely to win, was the last straw for the Governor and brought about his decision to resign. His resignation letter was already with the Home Office on 26 November, the day that the grant was being discussed by Tynwald. However, it was not until the next Tynwald, on 17 December, that anyone had any notion of his intentions.

After Tynwald passed the protest resolution, stating that demobilization donations should be provided by the British as part of military expenditure, and the day's business had been concluded, the governor begged a few moments of Tynwald's time. To a stunned legislature he announced his resignation, telling them, 'I have always had a great idea that people should not hang on to offices – more especially public offices after they have lost the spring of even a well-preserved middle age, which is all I can possibly lay claim to.'

He also cited his illness of 1915-16 and the fact that he felt that the task of reconstruction should fall to a younger man as reasons for his departure. No doubt he fully appreciated he was not the man to see the proposed reforms through and after some of the humiliations he had suffered in the preceding years, he had probably lost his appetite for the role. 'I don't say we have always thought the same way', was his pithy observation and he thanked his colleagues for their loyalty and patriotism during the recent trying times.

As the thunderbolt of his resignation became known, he received many tributes referring to his courtesy and kindliness; and many thanks were passed on to his wife for her charitable work. Despite having many opponents, he also had many admirers. As well as those who

Memorial to Lord Raglan at Onchan Church, which he attended while he was on the island.

owed their advancement and public office to him, there were those he had saved from income tax for many years and a ready made circle of friends and supporters in the Freemasons. He had been an affable and social Governor who was very interested in the island. He was an active member of the Natural History and Antiquarian Society and it is thanks to his initiative that Castle Rushen, in danger of crumbling into a ruin, was extensively restored and is still one of the island's main attractions.

Despite the fact that he and his policies had been ridiculed in both the Manx and British papers and that at times he was something of an embarrassment to his seniors at the Home Office, in the year of his retirement he was appointed GBE, the most senior rank in the Order of the British Empire, above the more prolific MBE and OBE etc.

The entrance to Castle Rushen, the ancient seat of power restored by Lord Raglan and where Ambrose Qualtrough faced trial.

It is unfortunate that Lord Raglan's poor grasp of finances and lack of diplomacy are what he is mainly remembered for. He had seen old age pensions as costly and unjustifiable; had advised hoteliers to sell up at the outbreak of war; was generally unsympathetic to the plight of the poor and had left social policy desperately neglected. Inadvertently he ensured that the reformist minority became a significant force simply by refusing to consider their proposals. To many, he would never be seen as anything other than a dictator whose resignation was greeted with great relief.

Samuel Norris lost no time in writing to the Prime Minister, Lloyd George. On behalf of the Redress, Retrenchment and Reform Campaign, he wrote of the hope that the new appointment would be for only a term of years as recommended by the Home Office Departmental Committee of 1911. He also asked that the new occupant should be highly competent and that he should be instructed to carry out the long since promised reforms in accordance with the wishes of the people.

The Keys also passed a resolution asking for the next Governor to be 'a statesman of experience in government and administration, one of proven capacity and in sympathy with progressive legislation'. The House also asked that the appointment be for a set number of years.

It took only four days for a reply to be received. It confirmed that the next appointment would indeed be limited to a given number of years and that the reforms that were interrupted by war would be expected to be dealt with as soon as possible.

Who the next Governor would be was a prolific topic of conversation. Hall Caine, the novelist, believed that the next Governor should be a Manxman. He proposed himself and put some considerable effort into a press campaign and persuading the Prime Minister. Samuel Norris did not support this idea; instead he felt that the close-knit island required a stranger as Governor, and a stranger who had been trained in the higher levels of the civil service. Despite this difference of opinion the two men remained friendly until the death of Hall Caine in 1933.

There were several rumours, including one saying the position had gone to George Barnes, a Labour member of the War Cabinet. Samuel Norris was told that someone who bore a great name in British Parliamentary history had been nominated, but when the name was submitted to the King, George V expressed his wish that all available positions should go to the soldiers who had just won the war.

Therefore, in 1919, another soldier, Major General William Fry, not a politician, became the next Governor. Serendipitously, Major General Fry was not the 'younger man' his predecessor had envisaged, as the two men were the same age. He also had some familiarity with the island as his wife was Manx and his father-in-law was for many years Speaker of the House of Keys. However, his limited term of seven years and his more liberal leanings were met with approval by the reformists. His general popularity was confirmed when in 1926, at the end of his term, the Keys recommended his term be extended, an offer that was not taken up by either the Home Office or the 68-year-old Fry.

One of the successes of Lord Raglan's tenure had been the efficient

KNOCKALOE CAMP
Knockaloe Farm served as
an internment camp for
over 20,000 German Civilians
interned during the period of
the Great War 1914 - 1918.

Sign at Knockaloe Farm.

and profitable running of the camps. However, once the war ended, these needed to be dissolved. Of the tens of thousands of internees, only about 3000 were actually allowed to remain in Britain. Those who had British wives and families stayed in the camps until their fates had been decided and their appeals heard. It was October 1919 by the time the camps were finally empty and, with very few successful appeals, most of the prisoners were deported. Some British wives followed and risked being subjected to anti-war and anti-British feeling after four years of anti-German prejudice. Many other wives stayed in Britain, preferring separation and often divorce.

The previous May there had been a particularly sad story regarding one of the internees who was faced with repatriation.

Fredrick Brandauer was interned in the Douglas Camp. At the age of 56, he had made a fortune as a steel pen manufacturer. He had lived in England for about thirty years and was naturalized in 1895. However, his sister still lived in Stuttgart and was married to General von Schorer.

In the early years of the twentieth century Brandauer returned to Germany. He was to move back to England a few years later, but he had let his British nationality lapse. He never married and, despite being relatively young, he was significantly disabled. He could not hear

Inside the Douglas camp. Courtesy of Manx National Heritage.

and was unable to walk unassisted, but at least his money helped him in the camp as it allowed him to pay for 'privilege' status.

The camp had three separate sections: the ordinary camp, the Jewish camp, and the privilege camp. About 400-500 lived in the privileged section. By paying 10s per week, two or three internees could secure a small hut between themselves. For £1 per week an internee could have his own hut and was allowed to have servants. About a hundred men from the ordinary camp found employment in the privilege camp in this way.

Brandauer was one of those lucky enough to have a valet, Frank Raab, who came with him from England. In April 1918 Brandauer received a letter that greatly upset him. He was informed that he was to be repatriated, but he had no wish to go back to Germany. He was excused on this first occasion, but three weeks later it was fully intended that he would be sent back and there would be no appeal. Fearing that he would not be physically fit enough to endure the journey and that there would be nobody to look after him if he did return, as it was not intended that his valet would go with him, he took the only course of action he believed open to him and committed suicide.

If one suicide was not tragic enough, the news of a second suicide soon followed. The second one, though, did not take place on the Isle of Man but in London. Fredrick Schramm, a German who had been naturalized, was found to have shot himself after hearing of the death of Brandauer. Schramm had worked with Brandauer and had been the foreign correspondent of Brandauer's company. It was said that he was

The graves of Turkish prisoners near Knockaloe.

very attached to Brandauer and had kept in touch. Like Brandauer, he was also said to be very fond of England.

Brandauer's actions were extreme, but after several years of being a prisoner in what many regarded as their own country, the future in another country that had just lost a war must have seemed very bleak.

The story of Hozinger, another internee, however, could not have been more different. He made a success of his new life. He had started a sock knitting workshop in his hut at Knockaloe and by 1920 he had a new knitting factory in Hamburg. Clearly he never forgot his time on the island, as his trademark was the three legs of Man.

Just as the camps had to be dissolved, it might have been expected that once Major General Fry had been sworn in as Governor on 3 April 1919 that he would dissolve the House of Keys. The House was the same one that had been elected in 1913 and, owing to the war was overdue for new elections. It was also one way to begin the reform programme that was expected of the new Governor.

In fact it would be November before the first post-war elections were held. Samuel Norris and four representatives of the Labour Party were among the seventeen new members. Deemster Moore, whose job it was to swear in all members at the beginning of the new session, remarked that he had never seen 'so many new faces' entering a new House. Only three years before he had sent Samuel Norris to jail.

Strangely, Samuel Norris, despite his clear political views and ability to poll the most votes, did not stand as a Labour Party candidate. However, he was much respected by his Labour colleagues and they were as disappointed as he was when he lost his seat to them in 1929. He was a victim of plumping. If there is more than one MHK to an area, each voter can have more than one vote. Sometimes supporters of a particular candidate will 'plump' to vote for just one in a bid to ensure that candidate is elected. Samuel Norris told his supporters not to 'plump' for just him and unfortunately he lost his seat by four votes. However, he returned to the Keys four years later.

Despite the presence of the Labour Party, the island continued to operate without party politics. Although seats gained in the name of the Labour Party were never numerous, the progressive nature of the new House after the 1919 election, with the help of a like-minded Governor, brought in many reforms. Perhaps most pleasing to Samuel Norris after his years of campaigning, was the introduction of old age pensions in 1920.

Elijah Oliver, who had been released from prison, returned to the island, where he continued to preach and speak publically about the lack of spiritualism in many churches. He also condemned the evil of gambling, spoke of the need for reform and, on a subject close to his heart, called for the abolition of conscription. He put himself up for election in 1919 and 1934. He gained a commendable number of votes but they were not enough to secure a seat and ultimately he left the island, dying in 1960 at Letchworth, in Hertfordshire.

Ambrose Qualtrough, who had gone to prison rather than pay a fine and who had been one of Lord Raglan's greatest critics, was re-elected in 1919 and 1924. Like Samuel Norris, he lost in 1929 after twenty-two years of service. Also, like Norris, he returned to the House in 1934 but died suddenly in May 1936.

The Great Laxey Mine, which had been struggling for many years, limped along until 1920. Laxey's lead had found a ready market but deposits from abroad had driven the price down. Industrial action by employees, led by the Workers' Union, calling for insupportably high wages finally closed the mine and later attempts to revive the industry were ultimately unsuccessful.

Reverend Copeland-Smith, one person who had risen to the challenge of the war years and successfully made a positive and immediate difference to the lives of many, was able to continue his vision. He believed that projects such as his industries would be part of the future of the island as the holiday trade was not necessarily sustainable.

At the end of the war he continued his Manx Industries as a commercial venture, with himself as director. Unfortunately disaster struck in April 1921 when his factory in Douglas caught fire. Shortly afterwards he had to file for bankruptcy. No doubt very disappointed, he left the island for the United States in 1922.

Considering how far-sighted his view of tourism was, the island probably lost more than it realized when Copeland-Smith left. Holiday makers did return, but the season was never what it had been prior to the war. The financial woes of the 1920s and 1930s had not been foreseen, neither had another war or the cheap package foreign holidays of the 1970s and beyond. True to Copeland-Smith's prophecy, the holiday industry has declined on the island and though far from extinct, the viability of the island without its financial centre would be questionable.

There were many changes for the local people during the conflict. A great proportion of men had left to fight and in their place came thousands of prisoners. There were various changes to the law and new 'rules' suddenly made something that was part of everyday life, such as lighting the streets, illegal. Most of all, fortunes changed. New found wealth lived side by side with new found poverty and created tensions between social groups and polarised politics.

For those left behind on the Isle of Man, their story is one of conflict and divisions. The country people, generally seen as conservative, had the opportunity to become wealthy while the townsmen, generally seen as liberal, became bankrupt. That little help was offered to those suffering financially was seen as an injustice and, with the House of Keys having a majority of country members, despite the population figures for town and country being similar, the town dwellers felt they had little support. The redistribution of seats was another reform measure that had been asked for and would come about in the fullness of time.

The war became a brake on the reforms that had been recommended in the early part of the decade. It was an excuse for not acting on them, but it also strengthened the resolve of many, who through the hardships they suffered were keen to see change. It gave great impetus to the reform movement, but even without the war many of those changes could have come to fruition, albeit in a less dramatic fashion.

Dire need manifested itself in many instances of direct action, most of which, frustratingly, could have been avoided if it had not been for the personality of the Governor. Lord Raglan had a certain amount of power but he did not always use his power wisely. He did not seem to realize that the surest way to create civil unrest is to have the people hungry and unhappy.

With peace and a new Governor, many had hope for a brighter future. Indeed there would be many changes for the better that would come about, but change takes time and there were still many new challenges to face.

National memorial at St John's.

For the immediate future, though, the returning soldiers were received as heroes and a variety of receptions were held for them. For the 1165 Manxmen killed, their names would be engraved on the memorials that were erected over the next few years and still stand today.

Bibliography

Beckerson, J.
Holiday Isle: the Golden Era of the Manx Boarding House from the 1870s to the 1970s
Manx Heritage Foundation 2007

Shepherd, J.
The Life and Times of The Steam Packet
Ferry Publications 1994

Scarffe, A.
The Great Laxey Mine
Manx Heritage Foundation 2004

Corkhill, A.
Hostile Sea
Mannin Media 2013

Kniveton, G., et al
Douglas Centenary 1896-1996
The Manx Experience & Aldern Press 1996

Cowin, D.
Douglas Isle of Man a History and Celebration
Frith Book Company Ltd 2004

Sargeaunt, B.E.
The Isle of Man and The Great War
Brown & Sons 1920

Cresswell, Y. (Ed)
*Living with the Wire, Civilian Internment in the Isle of Man During
Two World Wars*
Manx National Heritage 2010

West, M.
*Island at War, the Remarkable Role Played by the Small Manx
Nation in the Great War 1914-18*
Manx Heritage 1986

Norris, S.
Manx Memories and Movements
Manx Heritage Foundation 1994

Winterbottom, D.
Governors of the Isle of Man since 1765
Manx Heritage Foundation 2012

Belchem, J. (Ed)
*A New History of the Isle of Man Volume V. The Modern Period
1830-1999*
Liverpool University Press 2000

Sources

Mona's Herald

12 August 1914	14 April 1915	12 January 1916
26 August 1914	05 May 1915	19 January 1916
09 September 1914	12 May 1915	26 January 1916
16 September 1914	19 May 1915	02 February 1916
30 September 1914	26 May 1915	09 February 1916
04 November 1914	09 June 1915	01 March 1916
18 November 1914	16 June 1915	08 March 1916
02 December 1914	30 June 1915	19 April 1916
30 December 1914	29 September 1915	10 May 1916
	17 November 1915	12 July 1916
	08 December 1915	11 October 1916
	22 December 1915	18 October 1916
		08 November 1916
		22 November 1916

* * *

21 February 1917	20 March 1918
14 March 1917	24 April 1918
28 March 1917	01 May 1918
04 April 1917	03 July 1918
11 July 1917	10 July 1918
29 August 1917	28 August 1918
	16 October 1918

Peel City Guardian

15 August 1914	16 January 1915	01 January 1916
21 November 1914	24 April 1915	05 February 1916
05 December 1914	15 May 1915	04 March 1916
12 December 1914	12 June 1915	18 March 1916
26 December 1914	03 July 1915	13 May 1916
	10 July 1915	08 July 1916
		21 October 1916
		18 November 1916

*   *   *

31 March 1917	04 May 1918
12 May 1917	06 July 1918
07 July 1917	20 July 1918
	14 September 1918

Ramsey Courier

11 September 1914	23 April 1915	14 January 1916
25 September 1914	14 May 1915	21 January 1916
23 October 1914	28 May 1915	28 January 1916
30 October 1914	04 June 1915	18 February 1916
06 November 1914	11 June 1915	10 March 1916
20 November 1914	10 September 1915	20 April 1916
04 December 1914		06 June 1916
18 December 1914		20 October 1916

*   *   *

25 May 1917	08 March 1918
15 June 1917	22 March 1918
06 July 1917	12April 1918
10 August 1917	03 May 1918
31 August 1917	
02 November 1917	

Isle of Man Times

24 October 1914	04 March 1916	12 May 1917
	15 April 1916	02 June 1917
	11 November 1916	

*   *   *

23 February 1918
17 April 1918
04 May 1918
14 September 1918
21 September 1918

Isle of Man Examiner

05 September 1914	03 April 1915	01 January 1916
26 September 1914	17 April 1915	22 January 1916
31 October 1914	01 May 1915	29 January 1916
07 November 1914	15 May 1915	04 March 1916
14 November 1914	22 May 1915	18 March 1916
21 November 1914	05 June 1915	08 April 1916
19 December 1914	12 June 1915	13 May 1916
	03 July 1915	27 May 1916
	17 July 1915	17 June 1916
	14 August 1915	24 June 1916
	04 December 1915	08 July 1916
	25 December 1915	22 July 1916
		19 August 1916
		21 October 1916
		28 October 1916
		04 November 1916

*   *   *

Isle of Man Examiner - continued

24 February 1917	23 February 1918
31 March 1917	30 March 1918
05 May 1917	27 April 1918
17 May 1917	04 May 1918
26 May 1917	11 May 1918
16 June 1917	06 July 1918
07 July 1917	03 August 1918
04 August 1917	07 September 1918
11 August 1917	21 September 1918
15 September 1917	02 November 1918
03 November 1917	

Index